Exogenous versus Endogenous Governance of Open Collaborative Innovation Communities:

An Experimental Investigation

Niclas Störmer

Exogenous versus Endogenous Governance of Open Collaborative Innovation Communities:

An Experimental Investigation

Cuvillier Verlag Göttingen
Internationaler wissenschaftlicher Fachverlag

Bibliografische Information der Deutschen Nationalbibliothek

Die Deutsche Nationalbibliothek verzeichnet diese Publikation in der Deutschen Nationalbibliografie; detaillierte bibliografische Daten sind im Internet über http://dnb.d-nb.de abrufbar.

1. Aufl. - Göttingen : Cuvillier, 2013

Zugl.: (TU) Hamburg-Harburg, Univ., Diss., 2013

978-3-95404-590-7

© CUVILLIER VERLAG, Göttingen 2013

Nonnenstieg 8, 37075 Göttingen

Telefon: 0551-54724-0

Telefax: 0551-54724-21

www.cuvillier.de

1. Auflage, 2013

Gedruckt auf umweltfreundlichem, säurefreiem Papier aus nachhaltiger Forstwirtschaft.

978-3-95404-590-7

Acknowledgments

They say you have to stand on shoulders of giants to progress scientifically. Beyond the works of many researchers to build on I had many shoulders to stand and lean on while writing this thesis.

First, I want to express deep gratitude to my doctoral supervisor Prof. Dr. Herstatt for giving me the opportunity to carry out my research under excellent working conditions at the TU Hamburg-Harburg from day one.

I would like to thank my fellow research comrades. The many fruitful discussions and critical questions were always valuable and helped me gain new insights. Among those I especially want to thank two people: First Sarah, who not only shared an office but much laughter with me and second Tim, who seemed to have read every paper and shared all the insights with me.

I want to thank my friends, who enriched my life beyond the thesis. I especially want to thank Matthias for planting the seed of scientific curiosity during our all night long discussions as my roommate during university studies. I also want to thank Hendrik for taking me out of the academic ivory tower when needed, to enjoy things beyond work.

I am very grateful to have met Anna just at the beginning of this thesis. You have made the last years much more fulfilling.

Finally I want to thank my mother for her unconditional support in every situation of life and for always encouraging me to take a leave of absence from my job to write this thesis. I owe gratefulness to my sister, the full-time scientist in the family: For answering questions at any time of the day, but more so for being the greatest sister one could imagine.

Writing this thesis has been a satisfying, exciting and great experience. Without any doubt, I would do it all over again!

CONTENTS

List of Figures

List of Tables

List of Abbreviations

Content-specific abbreviations

CPRs	common-pool resources
IAD	institutional analysis and development (framework)
MOI	men on the inside
OCI	open collaborative innovation
OSS	open source software
R&D	research and development
TCE	transaction cost economics

General abbreviations

cf.	compare
e.g.	for example (exempli gratia)
et al.	and others (et alii)
vs.	versus

Mathematical abbreviations

ANOVA	analysis of variance
B	coefficient of regression
CFA	confirmatory factor analysis
df	degrees of freedom
MANCOVA	multivariate analysis of covariance
MANOVA	multivariate analysis of variance
N	number of observations
p	p-value
R^2	coefficient of determination
Std.	standard
SE	standard error
VIF	variance inflation factor
ηp^2	partial eta-squared
ß	standardized coefficient of regression

1 INTRODUCTION

"Throughout history corporations have organized themselves according to strict hierarchical lines of authority. Everyone was a subordinate to someone else – employees versus managers, marketers versus customers, producers versus supply chain subcontractors, companies versus the community. There was always someone or some company in charge, controlling things, at the 'top' of the food chain. While hierarchies are not vanishing, profound changes in the nature of technology, demographics, and the global economy are giving rise to powerful new models of production based on community, collaboration, and self-organization rather than on hierarchy and control."
(Tapscott & Williams, 2008: 1)

Is the way firms are organized outdated? Do firms have to part with the concept of hierarchical business organization in order to stay innovative and create value?

The study of organization and order within business corporations has been of great interest throughout history. Since Max Weber stated: "A fully developed bureaucratic apparatus compares with other organizations exactly as does the machine with the non-mechanical modes of production." (Weber, 1978: 973).[1] Therefore the organization, that is, the mode of creation of value within a company becomes a crucial competitive advantage. If, as implied by the introductory quotation, firms are faced with a paradigm shift to a new mode of organization, what lessons are to be learned to sustain the competitive advantage? The emergence of a new model of organization especially refers to the topic of innovation. For one thing "[e]veryone knows that innovation is a core business necessity." (Chesbrough, 2006: xiii). Another reason is that the nature of innovation as a combination of a new idea and its implementation (Rickartds, 1985) makes the innovation process particularly exposed to the paradigm shift. A nearly endless pool of creativity, embodied through volunteers interconnected via the internet and tools like search engines to tap endless amount of knowledge prove to be a strong source for innovation. The rise and application of concepts like open innovation, the opening of the innovation process, is an answer to

---

[1] Today the term bureaucratic mainly has a negative connation, signalling restraining effects for the performance of an organisation. Weber's original definition of bureaucracy however, referred to the general organization in the broad sense (cf. Adler, 2011).

the question raised at the beginning of this introduction. Firms have already started to part from the classical concept of a hierarchical business organization when it comes to innovation. The change from a "producer's model" of innovation to an open collaborative one is already well underway (Baldwin & von Hippel, 2011). However, many questions concerning this new model still need to be answered.

Open innovation is a wide field, involving various areas and perspectives. One intriguing phenomenon is the success of communities of volunteers creating innovative outcomes over the internet, such as open source software or *Wikipedia*. Communities of volunteers, so called open collaborative innovation (OCI)[2] communities, have risen outside the boundaries of firms and are different from business organizations in the sense that they are not mainly profit driven. However, they have considerable success in taking market share from profit oriented firms as the examples of the operating system *Linux* vs. *Microsoft Windows* and *Wikipedia* vs. *Encyclopedia Britannica* show. Not only because of their success, but also because of their implications for theory and practice have such communities raised large research interest (West & Lakhani, 2008). Different aspects have caught the attention of scholars, such as investigating communities as a new model of innovation creation (cf. Lee & Cole, 2003) or motives and characteristics of members of such communities (cf. Jeppesen & Frederiksen, 2006). A lot of attention has been paid to the question of governance of such communities. Some authors see the issue of organization and governance as one of the most important question for understanding such communities (Baldwin & Clark, 2006; Lerner & Tirole, 2002). Important, because governance within communities is different to the classical market or hierarchy paradigm, and may represent a new mode (Demil & Lecocq, 2006) and is also a necessary ingredient to create an organizational climate to attract volunteers for the community (Shah, 2006; Markus, 2007).

Especially in the field of open source software (OSS) researchers have investigated the mechanisms by which such communities govern themselves in order to achieve direction, control and coordination among community members (Markus, 2007). Recently, a growing number of firms make use of collaborative communities by sponsoring them (O'Mahony & West, 2005; Shah, 2006). A topic which promises new insights, as it has been of less interest so far:

---

[2] For a detailed definition of open collaborative innovation (OCI) communities see Chapter 2.2.

"There has been much less research on how firms use communities where they have limited control, which might even jeopardize their competitive advantage, as part of their business models." (Dahlander, Frederiksen, & Rullani, 2008: 116)

The emergence of firms shifts the focus from self-governance of volunteers to external, firm-initiated, governance of communities. This dissertation centers on the question, how a community of self-governed volunteers reacts to the influence of a firm, specifically through exogenous, firm-initiated governance.

1.1 Research objective and approach

If firms interact with communities they can choose different modes of interaction ranging from a loose affiliation to the foundation of own communities. To great extent different modes of firms' involvement depend on the business model of the firm (Dahlander & Magnusson, 2008). A firm that regards a community as one source among many for innovation and creativity is likely to interact differently than a firm that regards the value generated within the community as its major business. For that reason one has to conclude that there is not just one firm-community interaction, but many modes and configurations.

It is evident that the goals of profit oriented firms and communities of volunteers are not inevitably the same which can result in considerable tension (West & O'Mahony, 2008). Therefore the question of governance is central within the relationship of firm and community, since a large number of involved parties with diverse objectives, capabilities and involvement come together (Dahlander et al., 2008).

One key strategic issue for firms is "[...] how to attract the participation of a broad community of contributors, and then how to sustain their participation over time." (Chesbrough & Appleyard, 2007: 68). The way governance is structured in sponsored communities, that is, how work is organized and activities are controlled, will influence intrinsic motivation of volunteers to contribute (Jeppesen & Frederiksen, 2006). Negative reactions by volunteers are reported if a firm executes too much control and unfair ownership demands (Shah, 2006). Firms are aware of such challenges and try to counter it by legitimizing such decisions in letting volunteers participate by making the governance accessible (West & O'Mahony, 2008) (see also O'Mahony & West, 2005).

While the realization that participation in procedural processes seems indispensable, to date little is known about the precise effects of participation vs. no participation on the community. Field and experimental research from other fields, namely common-pool resources (CPRs) such as fishing grounds, provide evidence that externally imposed rules may crowd out endogenous cooperative behavior (Ostrom, 2000a) and preferences (Cardenas, 2004) thereby possibly negatively impacting intrinsic motivation (Frey, 1994). Valuable insights can be gained from these findings. However, open collaborative innovation (OCI) communities differ in many ways from the CPRs environment, for instance the specific nature of innovative work and contextual factors like communication over the internet. I therefore believe it to be worthwhile to investigate the question how a community of volunteers creating innovative outcomes copes with the influence of external regulation by an authoritarian institution like a firm.

It comes down to the question whether firms should impose governance rules on a community or rather leave it to itself by relying on self-governance. The aim of any OCI community is to produce (innovative) beneficial outcomes. Such a goal can only be reached if certain preconditions or influential key factors (e.g. motivation of participants, conflict resolution within the community) are fulfilled. Therefore the main research question that needs to be answered is how the choice between endogenous and exogenous governance rules affects such key factors.

This question is studied empirically using an experimental approach to directly manipulate exogenous vs. endogenous governance rules. The analyses of the empirical studies link quantitative and qualitative data. Such an approach, also known as triangulation blends a variety of data and methods in order to "[...] capture a more complete, holistic, and contextual portrayal of the unit(s) under study." (Jick, 1979: 603). To achieve a holistic view to the extent possible, further research questions are derived from the guiding one. Depending on these research questions hypotheses are developed and appropriate analyses are chosen. This leads to three interconnected studies, answering five research questions by employing three separate sources of data.

The first study addresses the effect of exogenous vs. endogenous governance rules on key factors, namely motivation, conflict and perceived justice of community members by analyzing self-reported quantitative data.

The second study investigates the association of these factors with the behavior and performance of a community. This is achieved by the quantitative analysis of interaction frequencies and performance measures.

The third study explores three further questions, employing a content analysis of community interaction. First, the reaction of a community to the exposure of exogenous vs. endogenous governance rules is investigated. Second, the type of governance a community chooses, contrasting 'closed' vs. 'open' types, is examined. Third, the emergence of rules within the community is observed.

1.2 Structure of dissertation and research approach

To answer the guiding research question, how key factors (e.g. motivation, conflict, justice) of an OCI community are influenced by exogenous vs. endogenous governance rules, this thesis consists of seven chapters. This chapter, **chapter 1**, initially presents the overall research interest and the guiding research question.

Chapter 2 gives an overview of the context of this thesis by describing open collaborative innovation (OCI) communities as a phenomenon of open innovation. A particular focus is placed on how such communities organize and govern themselves by reviewing prior work and concepts. Furthermore the relation of firms with OCI communities is set out and examined.

Chapter 3 explores existing theories explaining economic governance, more specifically governance of communities. I define the term of governance which is central within this thesis. Furthermore a theoretical frame, namely the Institutional Analysis and Development (IAD) framework is described. This theoretical framework is important with regard to the design of the experiment, as expected relationships for the formulation of research hypotheses are based on it.

I start **Chapter 4** formulating five research questions which shall be answered by three empirical studies. The second part explains the choice for an experimental method followed by a review of the methodology. The rest of the chapter describes the framework and its different components for the experiment. A major element includes the formulation of research hypotheses, which comprises the review of existing theories.

The detailed design and procedure of the empirical study is laid out in **chapter 5**. This includes a detailed description of the experimental setup, as well as instructions and the data collection.

Chapter 6 is devoted to the analysis of the experiment. At the beginning of the chapter the quantitative data sample is examined to meet assumptions for the following statistical analyses. The rest of the chapter is divided into three separate, but interconnected studies. Study 1 investigates the effects of different governance modes on key factors, namely motivation, conflict and justice within an OCI community via statistical analysis. Study 2 explores the effects of these factors on the behavior and overall performance of an OCI community. The chapter concludes with a qualitative investigation, study 3, exploring the reactions of the community to different modes of governance and the emergence of self-governance.

Finally, **chapter 7** concludes with a summary of findings. The summary is completed by a discussion of limitations of the findings, followed by implications for research and management.

2 PHENOMENOLOGICAL BACKGROUND

What is open innovation? What defines an open collaborative innovation community? And how do firms and communities interact? These fundamental questions are discussed within the following chapter. Based on prior work of various researchers, this chapter aims at setting the scene for my own research.

2.1 Open Innovation

Until today, the dominant model of innovation has been a 'producers' model, where the most important innovations are invented by firms and supplied to consumers (Baldwin & von Hippel, 2011). Such a classical model is also described as a 'closed' (Chesbrough, 2003) or 'vertical' (Bogers & West, 2012) innovation paradigm, where firms control the complete process of innovation. By contrast the new model is described as an 'open innovation' model:

> "Open innovation is a paradigm that assumes that firms can and should use external ideas as well as internal ideas, and internal and external paths to market, as the firms look to advance their technology." (Chesbrough, Vanhaverbeke, & West, 2008: vii)

While this definition primarily focuses on the research and development (R&D) process of firms, the open innovation field has outgrown this narrow view, now representing many streams and perspectives (Gassmann, Enkel, & Chesbrough, 2010). According to Gassmann et al. different perspectives contribute to the field of open innovation, such as the spatial perspective focusing on the globalization of innovation, the structural perspective focusing on increased separation of innovation activities and the user perspective, integrating users into the innovation process. Other authors consider user innovation as a parallel stream to open innovation (West & Bogers, 2010). User innovation has gained much attention and considerable research already. One of the reasons for this is the fact, that examples of user innovation have been found long before the radical diffusion of the internet and were never limited to software (von Hippel, 2001). No matter where one stands in the discussion concerning the roots and streams within the field of open innovation, it can be stated that the field of open innovation is a fast growing research field. Especially since 2005, the number of published papers on open innovation has grown rapidly (Dahlander & Gann, 2010). A systematic review of the growing research on open innovation by Dahlander and Gann (2010) revealed that the different streams are rather fragmented and that collaboration of researchers across diverse teams is rather the exception than the rule (see also Lee, Herstatt, & Husted, 2012). Both studies reveal that user innovation is considered an important – if not the most important – stream within the field of open innovation. Users joining together to form a community to innovate have been given much attention by researchers, mainly because it is recognized that communities outside the boundaries of the firms play a decisive role in creating and disseminating innovations (West & Lakhani, 2008).

2.2 Community-based Innovation

Communities of volunteers developing products in an open collaborative manner are outstanding examples of the success of a particular application of the 'open innovation' model.[3] Especially in the field of open source software (OSS) products developed by such communities are shown to be competitive with commercial products. OSS communities are a special form of innovation communities (von Hippel, 2006). The characteristics of such communities are described as a group which develops a new solution or solves a problem over the internet (Dahlander & Wallin, 2006). Fleming (2007) highlights that work is done free of charge and all outcomes are freely revealed:

> "We define an open innovation community as a group of unpaid volunteers who work informally, attempt to keep their processes of innovation public and available to any qualified contributor, and seek to distribute their work at no charge." (Fleming & Waguespack, 2007: 166)

Members of such communities may be either individuals or firms (von Hippel, 2006). Raasch et al. (2009) point out, that the outcome of the collaborative work is in some form exploited, either "[...] that it is produced and sold on a market, integrated into

---

[3] Community-based innovation fits within the definition of open innovation by Chesbrough (West & Lakhani, 2008).

other products that are marketed, deployed during the development of such products or used for any other private or commercial purpose." (Raasch, Herstatt, & Balka, 2009: 383). This is important when making a distinction between collaborative innovation communities and other virtual communities of volunteers. Virtual communities exist in many forms, for example private or professional discussion groups on a variety of heterogeneous topics.[4] Inevitably, numerous overlapping terms for communities exist: "[...] innovation communities, knowledge producing communities, online communities, scientific communities, technical communities, user communities, virtual communities or communities of practice." (West & Lakhani, 2008: 224). However, such communities do not necessarily produce innovative outcomes according to the definition by Raasch et al., nor do they necessarily cover the innovation process as a whole. Table 1 gives an overview of an attempt to distinct OCI communities from other types of communities along different dimensions.

Within this dissertation project I solely focus on communities' collaboratively producing innovative outcomes, excluding virtual communities in the broader sense. I thus limit the scope according to the definition of West and Lakhani (2008), who define innovation communities as voluntary associations of actors who produce innovations that are brought to market. In order to use a clear and unified term I refer to such communities within this thesis as open collaborative innovation (OCI) communities. This term is strongly based on Baldwin and von Hippel (2011), who speak of open collaborative innovation.

The resounding success of applications like the operating system *Linux* and the browser *Mozilla Firefox* are living proof how OSS products gain market shares from conventional companies. The amazing success of OSS has captured scholarly interest for various reasons. First, it is surprising that a team of volunteers can compete with a highly organized team of professionals (Cheliotis, 2009). Second, the realization that the original assumption "[...] that a requirement to contribute one's innovation to a commons would lead inevitably to the destruction of incentives to innovate [...]" (von Krogh & von Hippel, 2006: 975) has been disproved. This deviation from the "self-interested-economic-agent paradigm" (Lerner & Tirole, 2001) raises the question about

---

[4] Attempts have been made to classify such virtual communities by different authors (cf. Hagel & Armstrong, 1997; Markus, 2002)

motives of volunteers in such communities. A question which has been investigated by different authors (cf. Lakhani & von Hippel, 2003; Füller, Jawecki, & Mühlbacher, 2007; Jeppesen & Frederiksen, 2006; Roberts, Il-Horn Hann, & Slaughter, 2006).[5]

A further question is whether the open source community model can be transferred beyond software. An expansion beyond software has been the rise of so called open content, where volunteers produce knowledge resources. *Wikipedia*, an encyclopedia assembled by articles of volunteers, is a prominent example. Less prominent ones are the co-development of goods such as music or films (cf. Cheliotis, 2009) or open science (cf. Hellström, 2003).

A further expansion is the application to tangible goods, so called open design (Vallance, Kiani, S., & Nayfeh, 2001). Raasch et al. (2009) show that the application to this field has already taken place, featuring products such as beverages, telephones and home entertainment equipment.[6]

Obviously, many differences between the production of software or movies and physical good exist. While software and cultural goods share a lot of features (Madison, Frischmann, & Strandburg, 2010), the difference between knowledge resources and physical goods is evident. Since tangible products involve costs for production, the OCI community model may not apply (Lee & Cole, 2003). However, a growing number of authors emphasize that many insights for other industries can be gained from the OSS model (cf. Ulhøi, 2004; Franke & Shah, 2003). Even though a direct transfer of the OSS model fails due differences between the goods, the diffusion beyond software has already taken place, as the mentioned examples show:

> "User innovation communities are by no means restricted to the development of information products like software. They also are active in the development of physical products, and in a very similar ways." (von Hippel, 2006: 103).

Considering definitions by the different authors mentioned, six main features of collaborative innovation (OCI) communities are apparent. First, members engage

---

[5] For an extensive overview about current research on motivation of volunteers in such communities see Chapter 4.3.2.1.

[6] The application to sports equipment, such as kite surfing, is a further example from this field (von Hippel, 2006). However, in this example the community does not necessarily communicate virtually.

voluntarily and free of charge. Second, they solely communicate over the internet. Third, they are associated by a common objective to create one solution or outcome. Fourth, the product of the work is either a public good or at least available for any contributor. Fifth, the product is exploited in either a commercial or private sense. Sixth, members of such communities are either individuals or firms.

Dimension	**OCI Community**	**Online Community**	**Community of Practice**
Objective	Common objective to create an outcome	Sharing of information, possible creation of outcome	Sharing of information, possible creation of outcome
Exploitation of outcome	Exploited either commercially or privately	Not necessary exploited	Not necessary exploited
Members	Volunteers with expert skills	Volunteers	Volunteers or professionals with shared expertise
Communication	Internet based	Internet based	Internet based or face to face
Type of task	Complex tasks	Ranging from simple to complex	Ranging from simple to complex
Structure of work	Collaborative, work is based on predecessor	Independent work	Some collaborative aspects
Parts of the innovation process (Ideation, Development, Production, Marketing)	All parts of the process are covered	Only parts of the process are covered (e.g. just support for a product, or ideation for new ones)	Only parts of process are covered

Table 1: Distinction of an OCI community with other forms of communities along different dimensions

2.2.1 Governance of open collaborative innovation communities

The phenomenon of open collaborative innovation (OCI) communities has also raised the question how these communities succeed in governing themselves. Specifically, how they manage to coordinate work of many volunteers and how they create the wider institutional conditions to flourish as a community (de Laat, 2007b). In the following section I try to identify the mechanisms by which OCI communities solve the challenges of coordination, referring to the work of various authors.

The issue of governance of OCI communities is important, because governance within such communities is different to the classical market or hierarchy paradigm, and may represent a new mode (Demil & Lecocq, 2006). Furthermore the exchange within these communities is not that of physical goods but rather of "nonrivalrous and nonexcludable" knowledge resources (Madison et al., 2010). Some authors see the question of organization and governance as one of the key questions for understanding such communities, (Baldwin & Clark, 2006; Lerner & Tirole, 2002) and also as a necessary ingredient to create an organizational climate to attract participants (Shah, 2006; Markus, 2007). While there is consensus that governance is an important issue, no clear definition of governance in OCI communities has emerged to date (Ying & Salomo, 2011).[7] Within the context of OSS communities, different authors have made attempts to define the term governance. Demil and Lecocq (2006) define governance as focusing on the transactions of actors within the community.

> "A governance structure is an institutional framework regulating transactions between actors." (Demil & Lecocq, 2006: 149)

The definition by Markus (2007) specifies what can be understood by regulating transactions:

> "Thus, OSS governance can be defined as the means of achieving the direction, control, and coordination of wholly or partially autonomous individuals and organizations on behalf of an OSS development project to which they jointly contribute." (Markus, 2007: 152)

---

[7] The lack of a clear definition of governance is not limited to the field of OCI communities, but seems to hold true for the term governance in general (see Chapter 3.1 for more detail).

In the same manner Bonaccorsi and Rossi (2003) raise the question of coordination, in order to understand governance within OSS communities:

> "The spontaneous, decentralized functioning of the Open Source community represents a challenge to many current notions of co-ordination. How is it possible to align the incentives of several different individuals without resorting to property rights and related contracts? How is it possible to specify everyone's tasks without resorting to a *formal* hierarchical organization based on ownership of assets?" (Bonaccorsi & Rossi, 2003: 1244).

Considering these definitions governance within OCI communities addresses two main problems: First, coordination to reach one goal. Second, controlling and safeguarding interactions and relationships between individuals. These problems are conforming to governance issues of networks of firms, as described by Jones et al. (1997). According to the authors, such challenges are solved via different governance mechanisms. The same holds true for OCI communities, where researchers have investigated the mechanisms by which such communities solve the governance problems in order to achieve direction, control and coordination among community members (Markus, 2007).

Mechanisms of governance

Numerous mechanisms of governance have been identified by various authors. As the overview in Table 2 shows, overlaps between identified mechanisms by different scholars exist. In order to clarify the terms I have harmonized the different mechanisms to different clusters. Even though no perfect one-to-one mapping was always possible, six different clusters emerge (see Table 2). The first is (1) *modularization* which incorporates splitting up the project in different modules. The modularity proves to be a lever to incentivize volunteers and decreases free-riding (Baldwin & Clark, 2006). A second cluster is (2) *hierarchy & roles*, which refers to roles such as project leader or administrator. The way decisions are made within such communities is reflected within the third cluster, the definition of a (3) *decision process*. Decisions within these communities are concerned with different domains, such as the appointment of leadership (de Laat, 2007a) or the release control of products (Shah, 2006). Many communities have strict rules how to communicate, which is reflected in (4) *communication rules* regarding tool related issues such as mailing lists or procedures about what information is shared. A fifth cluster defines who owns the work of the community due (5) *property rights*, which are often incorporated in different licenses. The final cluster is concerned with how order is achieved, more specifically how the compliance with governance mechanisms is achieved. Different (6) *monitoring* mechanisms contribute to realizing this goal, for example by rules for conflict resolution.

Reference	Governance mechanisms	Description	Cluster
de Laat (2007a) – Governance of open source software: state of the art	Modularization	Splitting the project up in different modules	Modularization
	Division of Roles	Different roles regarding expertise and responsibilities	Hierarchy & Roles
	Delegation of decision-making	Centralized vs. Decentralized decision structure	Decision process
	Training and indoctrination	Entry conditions for new members, prove of knowledge and allegiance to the philosophy	Monitoring
	Formalization	Tools and procedures to communicate	Communication rules
	Autocracy/democracy	The way leadership is appointed	Decision process
Markus (2007) – The governance of free/open source software projects: monolithic, multidimensional, or configurational?	Ownership of assets	Intellectual property rights	Property rights
	Chartering the project	Statement about vision and goals	Monitoring
	Community management	Rules who can be member, what roles they can play	Hierarchy & Roles
	Software development process	Rules for operational tasks and release control	Decision process
	Conflict resolution and rule changing	Rules and procedures for resolving conflict	Monitoring

		and for creating new rules	
	Use of information and tools	Rules about how information will be communicated and managed	Communication rules
Shah (2006) – Motivation, Governance, and the Viability of Hybrid Forms in Open Source Software Development	Decision making rights Code control Mailing list	Right to alter code and domination over mailing list	Decision process
Capra, Francalanci, & Merlo (2008)– An Empirical Study on the Relationship Between Software Design Quality, Development Effort and Governance in Open Source Projects	Code Property rights Contribution of volunteers Project leadership (hierarchy) Working practices		Property rights Decision process Hierarchy & Roles
Bonaccorsi, Rossi (2003) – Why Open Source software can succeed: Open Source Software Developement	Leadership	Hierarchy with project leaders	Hierarchy & Roles
	Modularization	Splitting up the project	Modularization
	Communication tools	Mailing list, and knowledge databases	Communication rules
	Licences	Different licensing modes	Property rights

Table 2: Governance mechanisms by different authors and assignment to clusters

The different mechanisms relate to the two main governance problems (coordination and control) within OCI communities. The two objectives of governance, to coordinate and control transactions within communities, are strongly interrelated. Many mechanisms attribute to both objectives, for example defined decision processes help coordinating work but may as well mitigate conflicts between actors. The same holds true for communication rules. Restricting certain actors from communication (e.g. through closed mailing lists) may function as a coordination device, but attributes also to safeguarding certain sensitive information. Figure 1 gives an overview how the different mechanisms address the two main governance problems.

The mechanisms are institutionalized through rules (except for modularization, which is more concerned with the initial structure of a project), for example rules that describe the responsibilities and decision powers of certain roles or rules that describe how to communicate and who can join the community. In other words all described mechanisms are embodied through a diverse set of rules. These can be either explicit or implicit. Ostrom's extensive work in the field of governance of common-pool resources (CPRs) has led to a set of seven generic governance rules (Ostrom, 2005) which show extensive overlaps with the identified mechanisms in OSS communities (Schweik & Kitsing, 2010).[8] I am also well aware that many 'invisible' mechanisms of governance exist. Attributes like trust, solidarity and reciprocity allow for smooth interaction within communities lacking formal mechanisms. The importance of such informal mechanisms has been highlighted by different authors (cf. Lerner & Tirole, 2002; Bowles & Gintis, 2002).

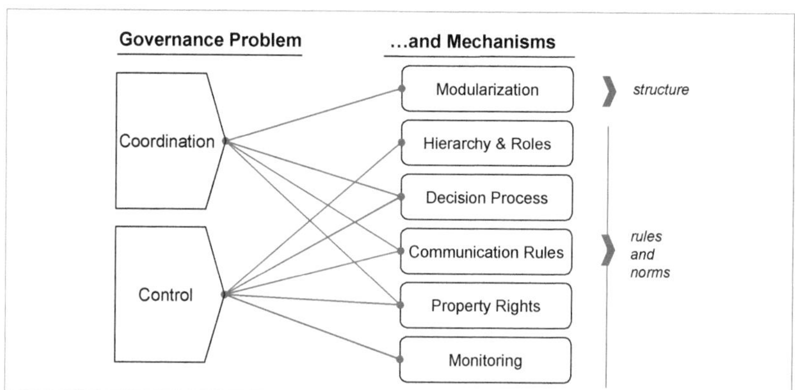

Figure 1: Mechanisms solving governance problems (adapted from Jones et al., (1997)

Governance as a dynamic process

Governance is seen as a dynamic process that evolves over time (Heide, 1994). Besides the identification of distinct mechanisms, the evolvement of governance in communities should be considered to fully understand. It is evident that communities

---

[8] For an extensive overview on Ostrom's work and how the generic rules fit within the context of OCI communities see chapter 3.3.1.

are not static, but grow and develop over time. At the same time, with increasing size and maturity of the community, the need for governance amplifies.

Lattermann and Stieglitz (2005) identify four clearly specifiable life cycle stages, with different modes of governance. The first stage, the *introduction stage*, is characterized by an informal structure based on trust and generic roles. The second stage, the *growth stage*, leads to a more formalized structure with formal communication rules, precisely different mailing lists and specialized roles such as release manager or interface designer. During the third stage, the *maturity stage*, former informal means like trust are replaced by more formal ones. The last stage, the *decline stage*, shows no new features of governance but rather a decrease of participation and output.

O'Mahony and Ferraro's (2007) analysis of the emergence of governance in OCI communities reveals different phases, from de facto governance to a stabilized system. The authors identify four phases: First, autocratic leadership emerges and is challenged. During the second phase, the autocratic leadership is transferred into formal authority, for example the separation of roles. Again, such formal authority may be challenged which leads to the third phase when democratic means are introduced to elect leaders. In the final stage, the community has a shared conception of formal authority and the means of legitimizing it.

In summary, the emergence of governance can be described as an evolution from informal norms to a more formal structure. During this quest authority emerges and is again countered by democratic means until social order, institutionalized by a governance system, is existent. While the emergence of social order is a vast field mainly reserved for sociologist and shall not be discussed in this dissertation project (cf. Greif, 1997; Streeck & Schmitter, 1985), I propose a further view. If a community has to settle on governance rules it undergoes a process integrating possibly diverse individual positions into a consensus – a process which is characterized as a group decision process. Group decision processes have been investigated comprehensively (cf. Kerr & Tindale, 2004; Kaplan & Miller, 1987). I consider the formation of endogenous governance by a group as a group decision process. Different preferences for diverse rules have to be integrated in one set of rules which is accepted by all. On the contrary, exogenous governance is characterized by exclusion of community members from any decision process, giving them no participation rights for designing such rules.

Interaction of governance and human behavior

The emergence of governance is a dynamic process, which is influenced and shaped by human behavior. Consequently, beyond identifying mechanisms and the evolution of governance, the aspect of interrelations between governance and psychological states, such as motivation, and resulting behavior, such as participation has been of interest (cf. Jeppesen & Frederiksen, 2006; Shah, 2006). Of interest, as human behavior is the key factor for a prospering community. Many different questions seem valuable when investigating the relations between governance and human behavior. One promising question is which effects diverse configurations of governance mechanisms have on aspects like motivation as an antecedent of performance (Markus, 2007). Lee and Cole (2003), for example investigated how certain governance mechanisms, specifically different property rights, motivate volunteers to participate. A second question is how volunteers who normally govern themselves react to exogenously indoctrinated governance. An important aspect for the motivation of volunteers is a feeling of freedom to choose (e.g. task, topic, time) (Dahlander et al., 2008). Pursuing this line of reasoning Markus (2007) suggests, "[...] one may hypothesize that OSS projects with governance characterized by greater degrees of democratic 'openness' [...] are more motivational." (Markus, 2007: 157). This proposition is supported by a study from West and O'Mahony (2008) who show that the degree of openness of a governance structure, more precisely the transparency and ability to influence it, affects the participation and attractiveness of a community. The question, how the possibility to shape the governance affects key factors such as motivation is even more justified, if account is taken of the growing influence of commercial firms on OCI communities. In order to secure property rights and their value capture firms are more likely to choose a 'closed' governance mode, depriving volunteers from extensive participation rights. The emergence of firms within the context of OCI communities thus raises the question how formerly self-governed groups of mainly altruistic individuals react to the influence of a profit oriented actor.

2.2.2 Firms and collaborative innovation communities

The growing success of OCI communities attracted the interest of firms and other institutions. While communities were originally founded via grassroots means by individuals, corporations nowadays often sponsor such communities (O'Mahony, 2007).

The foundation of communities by firms has become a common phenomenon, where the sponsoring firm plays a central role (West & Lakhani, 2008). The main purpose of any firm is to generate profits. Consequently, the rationales of firms to engage with OCI communities are driven mainly by economic and technological reasons (Bonaccorsi & Rossi, 2006). Economic reasons include cost benefits within the innovation process by exploiting the work of the community (Hawkins, 2004) or generating revenues by complementary services (Feller & Fitzgerald, 2002). Technological reasons include the promotion of certain standards (Fink, 2003) and the improvement of products through feedback (Hawkins, 2004). The emergence of firms raises new questions, since many of the described principles and features of OCI communities clash with the traditional requirements of profit oriented firms.

Lee and Cole (2003) highlight the differences between a firm-based and a community-based model of innovation (see also West & O'Mahony, 2008). Especially free revealing, that is, the voluntary publishing of innovation related information secrets (Harhoff, Henkel, & von Hippel, 2003), is likely to conflict with firms effort to protect their intellectual property. Consequently, sponsored communities may differ from 'classical' OCI communities by limiting the property rights through licensing (Shah, 2006). However, there are numerous examples of firms leaving the property rights with the community (cf. Lee et al., 2012; West & O'Mahony, 2008). Such behavior should be not interpreted as altruistic. Property rights are not given up for selfness reasons, but firms pursue different strategies that are consistent with traditional economic analysis (Hawkins, 2004). They may be more open, leaving the property rights with the community if they are likely to benefit from it. Such benefits are congruent with the mentioned economic reasons and include savings (Hawkins, 2004) or selling complementary services and products (Lerner & Tirole, 2002).

Strategies and mechanisms of firms to interact with OCI communities

Investigating firm-community interactions leads to the community strategy of a firm, that is, how they interact and make use of the community. Depending on a firm's business model (Dahlander & Magnusson, 2008) and variables, such as industry, firm or industry size and environment (Fosfuri, Giarratana, & Roca, 2011), different modes of a firm's involvement with communities emerge.

Dahlander and Magnusson (2008) identify three approaches how firms use communities. The first is (1) *accessing* communities in order to extend their resource base. According to Dahlander and Magnusson, such additional resources can be accessed by either establishing own communities to attract external volunteers to work immediate of the firm or by using existing communities. The second is (2) *aligning* the firm's strategy with the community. Again, two tactics can be used. First, adopting the licensing practice (that clarifies the ownership) of the community. Second, guiding the community to work on tasks that are of high relevance for the firm. A third is (3) *assimilating* the work of the community. This is done by devoting resources to the community to evaluate their work and by feeding-back non-strategic work developed by the firm to the community.

Fosfuri et al. (2011) taxonomy of firms' strategies towards communities includes four diverse strategies. While they focus on communities in a broader sense, not confining the focus on innovation communities but on communities that provide a reservoir of potential customers, many insights for the interaction between firms and OCI communities can still be gained. Fosfuri et al. define different strategies according to two dimensions. The first dimension is the congruence between the firm's and community values. If a firm and community share and support the same values high congruence can be stated. A low level of congruence does not necessarily indicate a conflict between community and firm values, but may indicate different prioritization of values. The second dimension is concerned with the power of a firm to influence the community. According to the authors, both dimensions are interdependent: For example, the influence of a firm may be determined by the commitment to the community values. Applying the two dimensions they define four different strategies, how a firm influences the identity and values of a community: (1) *Signaling* where the firm aligns itself with an existing community, (2) *identity-enhancing* where the firm actively contributes to and co-creates the community, (3) *identity-creation* where the firm is the main force in creating the identity of a community, (4) *avoiding* where the firm evades from the community. Therefore, avoiding can be seen as a 'none' strategy, since there is no overlap of firm's value and no influence of the firm (Fosfuri et al., 2011).

Alongside the identification of strategies authors have suggested different concrete measures and actions to implement such strategies. A common understanding is that firms have to invest resources to benefit from communities. Dahlander and Wallin

(2006) describe an approach where firms dedicate an employee – a 'man on the inside' (MOI) to engage with the community, that is, to participate and interact with the community, which allows influencing the direction of the community to some extent. A clarification of specific functions by which a 'man on the inside' influences a community has been described by Lee et al. (2012). Such important functions include the provision of expertise and the management of processes and relations between firm and community.

West and O'Mahony (2008) identify different design dimensions a firm can influence when sponsoring a community. The first dimension is concerned with the management of intellectual property rights. The second one deals with the organization of production within the community. The third one is concerned with governance of the community. According to the authors, firms` involvement influence these dimension in two ways. First by affecting the degree of transparency, that is, how open and public issues are being discussed in mailing lists or discussion boards. Second, influencing the degree of accessibility – "[...] the amount of control sponsors would relinquish to the community." (West & O'Mahony, 2008: 156). The design choices made by a firm reflect the tension between an aspiration for control and the need to attract volunteers. Firms generally are more willing to grant higher transparency than accessibility which indicates a strong desire for control (West & O'Mahony, 2008).

Considering the different strategies, mechanisms and design principles firms can apply in utilizing OCI communities, one has to conclude that there is not just one firm-community interaction, but many modes and configurations. Firms can choose between different approaches of interaction ranging from a loose affiliation to the foundation of own communities. A firm that regards a community as one source among many for innovation is likely to interact differently than a company that regards the value generated within the community as its major business. As for any strategic option, each choice has it potential advantages and disadvantages. For the best possible choice firms should be clear which objective they want to achieve by engaging with a community.

Overall, it is evident that the relationship of firm and community is a delicate issue – in particular because of the described conflict between a profit oriented 'closed' and a collective action 'open' model. A successful cooperation between firm and community requires merging these two models, namely the private investment and the collective action model, integrating the "best of both worlds" (von Hippel & von Krogh, 2003).

The importance of governance for firm and community relation

Investigating the relationship between firm and community by identifying different strategies and actions is closely linked to the issue of governance. While the structure of self-governed communities, that is, how work is organized and activities are controlled is already a complex issue (see Chapter 2.2.1) it becomes even more difficult with a firm's involvement. It has been stated that the goals of a community and a profit oriented firm are likely to be contradictory. As the number of actors and goals increases so does the need for governance. This observation applies to the interaction of firms and communities, since a large number of involved parties with diverse objectives, capabilities and involvements come together (Dahlander et al., 2008).

Not only does this complexity increase the demand for governance, but governance is the main mean of exerting power and influence. Property rights, control of information, setting of objectives are institutionalized and dealt with on the basis of governance rules. For firms it is important to understand that the configuration of governance of the community will determine how much influence and control they have. Just as firms invest in securing their products through patents and safeguarding exchanges through contracts, they have to define and structure their relationship with a community. Of course firms are well aware of this risk as the fear of knowledge drain shows (cf. Laursen & Salter, 2006). Applying established mechanisms of protection, for example patent law or contracts to the community, may be a first reflex. Especially as the distinction what is patentable and what is not has been changed recently, as the practice of business process patents shows (Walter & Möhrle, 2009). However, these mechanisms do not work when it comes to communities for different reasons. For one reason an OCI community consists of volunteers that are beyond the control of the firm. Enforcing property rights or non-disclosure violations of volunteers, who do not represent or belong to legal entities or whose full names are most likely not known, may be difficult for practical reasons. However, this line of reasoning has most likely no point, because it is not expected to ever happen. Installing a tight property rights regime is likely to scare off any volunteer participation. Therefore, a firm will not have a community in the first place. This takes us to next important point, the connection between governance and the attractiveness of the community for volunteers.

The connection between governance and motivation of volunteers has been already mentioned in the introduction, while stating my research objective. The way governance is structured in sponsored communities will influence intrinsic motivation of volunteers to contribute (Jeppesen & Frederiksen, 2006). Negative reactions by volunteers are reported if a firm executes too much control and unfair ownership demands (Shah, 2006). I already mentioned that firms are aware of such challenges and try to counter it by legitimizing the governance in letting volunteers participate in the decision process (West & O'Mahony, 2008) (see also O'Mahony & West, 2005). However, to date still little is known how successful such attempts are. It is of interest how participation vs. no participation of volunteers in creating the governance influences the characteristics of the community, more precisely the motivation and interaction behavior of community members. If clear cause and effect relationships of how participation or non-participation renders these factors are established, it is possible for firms to make decisions based on these finding. Decisions concerning the interaction with an OCI community by structuring the governance in a way to balance their desire for control, while at the same time creating a climate to attract and retain volunteers.

3 THEORETICAL FOUNDATIONS OF GOVERNANCE

Why do we need theory? In particular, what is the necessity for a theory with regard to this dissertation project? While this question may seem odd at first sight, the answer to this question helps to understand the purpose of theory and consequently this chapter. According to *The American Heritage Dictionary* a theory is defined as:

> "A set of statements or principles devised to explain a group of facts or phenomena, especially one that has been repeatedly tested or is widely accepted and can be used to make predictions about natural phenomena." (The American Heritage dictionary)

From this definition one important characteristic shall be highlighted. A theory allows making predictions about relationships – a pre-condition in order to design an empirical study and to formulate hypotheses. Furthermore the use of a suitable theory helps to center the right components to investigate. It therefore provides a clear focus, a theoretical domain that specifies what is at the center of investigation (e.g. differences across people, across organizations) (Feldman, 2004).

These two objectives, laying a base for predictions of relationships and providing a frame to focus on the right components, lie at the center of this chapter. However, I first discuss the term governance, as it is fundamental within this thesis.

3.1 Definition of the term Governance

The term 'governance' is widely used, incorporating the fields of politics, economy and society. It even reaches into the public debate – ongoing discussions about 'good governance' of public institutions and the establishment of a German commission of the corporate governance code[9] are recent examples. This application to dissimilar areas is reflected by the wide range of academic disciplines dealing with the topic of governance. As indicated by a review of academic research projects, the topic of governance is under examination by different academic disciplines ranging from political science to philosophy (with political science accounting for nearly 50%,

---

[9] The Government Commission appointed by Justice Minister September 2001 adopted the German Corporate Governance Code on February 26, 2002.

followed by law and economics) (Schuppert, 2008). However, the application of the term 'governance' to different disciplines does not contribute to more clarity, it rather blurs it, since the distinctness of it is reduced inevitable (Benz, Lütz, Schimank, & Simonis, 2007), making it a "confusing term" (Pierre & Peters, 2000). From the standpoint of scientific domains the theoretical roots of 'governance' can be traced back to political science and institutional economics (Benz et al., 2007). Referring to the works of Coase and Williamson the transaction cost economics introduced the concept of institutions to solve the coordination problem outside of markets via governance mechanism such as hierarchies (Lattemann, 2007).

Different disciplines and roots inevitably lead to different concepts of how to define governance. Rather than discussing numerous definitions I focus on economic governance, a much more specific term. I base this view on Dixit (2009) who defines three objectives for economic governance: (1) security of property rights, (2) enforcement of contracts and (3) collective action. This definition largely conforms to the definition of governance in OCI communities which was discussed in Chapter 2.2.1. Hence, I believe that the theory of economic governance provides a valuable theoretical base for my research.

3.2 Economic Governance

The challenge of communities to facilitate efficient coordination and safeguarding of the production process is not specific to OCI communities. These challenges are fundamental economic problems that apply to all interactions between firms or individuals. To investigate means how these interactions are supported and safeguarded is at the center of research on economic governance.

Economic governance has been of growing interest in the last decades, culminating in the Nobel Prize in economic sciences awarded to Elinor Ostrom and Oliver Williamson for their work on economic governance in 2009. In its reasoning, the Committee of the Royal Swedish Academy of Sciences argued, that economic governance is concerned with the best suited and efficient governance mechanisms, in particular set of rules, to support and protect the exchange and production of goods (Economic Sciences Prize Committee of the Royal Swedish Academy of Sciences, 2009). They add that the contributions by both laureates are complementary, Williamson focusing on transactions between and within firms that are not covered by detailed contracts, Ostrom focusing on common-pool resources (CPRs) and the problem of rule enforcement.[10]

Both works provide a theoretical base for this dissertation. Nevertheless economic governance is a wide field with different theories and concepts contributing to it. Williamson (2005) names four conceptual cornerstones of economic governance, namely governance, transaction costs, adaption and interdisciplinary science. All these concepts contribute to finding and studying feasible modes of organization to work out efficient transactions by alternative modes of governance (Williamson, 2005).

Ostrom speaks of an "interdisciplinary field" when studying economic behavior and outcomes (Ostrom, 2007). The wide range of disciplines dealing with the topic of governance, as mentioned in the previous chapter, is evidence of this. The statements of both laureates of the Nobel Prize highlight, that there is no one theory of economic governance. Rather different theories, concepts and frameworks contribute to an understanding how actors coordinate and safeguard their transactions. Which theories and concepts to apply are highly dependent on the perspective and specific research question. For example the level of analysis contrasting an organizational macro level or focusing on an individual micro level. Within this chapter I try to integrate different concepts and theories that relate to the specific research question of this thesis. I do so by briefly outlining the different conceptual cornerstones and making an attempt to link those to one framework (see Figure 2).

In order to do so, I focus on different components of a governance situation. Namely actors (e.g. individuals, firms) and the transaction taking place between the actors. I start with focusing on the transaction between actors resorting to the theory of transaction cost economics (TCE).

---

[10] Common-pool resources (CPRs) are resources which everybody has access to, for example fish stocks or drinking water (cf. Ostrom, 1999).

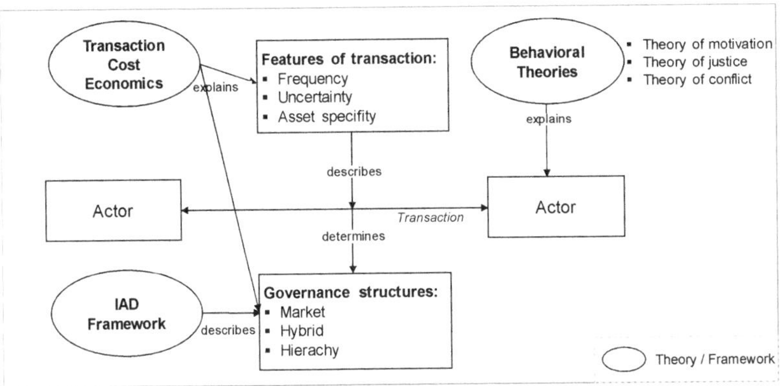

Figure 2: Theories and concepts and their relationship as applied within this thesis

Transaction cost economics

Transaction cost economics applies to a broad range of science topics and disciplines and has played a major role in the development of organizational theory, strategic management and political economy (Carroll & Teece, 1999). Williamson (1989) argues that TCE tries to answer questions about economic organization, that is, different forms of organizations, the different purpose of such organizational forms and on what features in human, technology and process respects these organizational forms rely on. Transaction cost theory can be applied for three levels of analysis: (1) a study of the overall structure of a firm; (2) activities of a firm, asking which should be performed inside or outside; (3) how human assets are organized (Williamson, 1981). Such inquiries relate exactly to question raised in the introduction, whether firms have to develop a new model of innovation. Consequently transaction cost economics seems a lens worthwhile to apply.

Using this lens the transaction is the central unit of analysis (Commons, 1990). Transactions take place when services or goods are exchanged across a separable interface; the costs associated with this exchange are the cost of a transaction, similar to the friction (loss of energy) in mechanical systems (Williamson, 1981). The cost relate to the features of transactions, which can be described by "[...] (1) the frequency with which they recur, (2) the degree and type of uncertainty to which they are subject, and (3) the condition of asset specifity." (Williamson, 1989: 142). Williamson (1989) details what is to be understood by uncertainty and asset specifity:

Uncertainty is broken down into primary uncertainty or risk, for example random acts of nature, and secondary uncertainty or hazards, that is, uncertainty resulting from behavior. To reduce this second type of uncertainty is part of successful governance structures.

Asset specifity refers to which degree an asset can be redeployed to alternative use without a loss of value. Asset specifity has many forms, for example human assets (certain skills) or physical assets (specialized components to produce one good).

Based on these features of a transaction firms chose different organizational designs. Their organizational design is chosen to minimize the transaction costs (Roberts & Greenwood, 1997). Therefore the organizational design can be seen as the dependent variable influenced by asset specifity, uncertainty and frequency functioning as independent variables (Shelanski & Klein, 1995). For example the choice between a market and a firm organization largely depends on the asset specifity: if an asset is nonspecific, the market (buying the product externally) provides benefits like scale economies or risk-pooling benefits, whereas if the asset becomes more specific the governance cost increase and internal production becomes more efficient (Williamson, 1981).

Therefore firms' organizational design can be seen as a governance structure (Williamson, 1998) which allows for the description of three archetypes of governance structure, namely markets, hybrids and hierarchies:

> "The economics of governance makes three basic governance structure distinctions: classical markets (simple spot-market exchange), hybrid contracting (of a long-term kind), and hierarchies (firms, bureaus)." (Williamson, 2005: 7)

According to Williamson (1998) each of the generic governance structures has salient differences concerning the (1) incentive intensity, (2) administrative control, (3) adaption, and (4) contract law. For example markets are characterized by high levels of incentives and lower administrative control whereas hierarchies are described by the exact opposite. Governance structures do not exist per se but are made of detailed governance rules. Such rules managing the transactions are embodied in institutions:

> "Institutions are the rules of the game in a society or, more formally, are the humanly devised constraints that shape human interactions. In consequence they structure incentives in human exchange, whether political, social, or economic." (North, 1990: 3)

Institutions are existent in various forms, such as business organizations, laws or governments. Understanding the nature and mechanisms of such institutions is the key question of economic governance.

Another important aspect of TCE is human behavior, also referred to as the second layer of TCE (Groenewegen, 1996). This second layer takes into account the importance of human behavior. Williamson (1981) highlights two behavioral realizations about human nature: (1) agents are subject to bounded rationality, that is, they cannot process all information of complex problems, and therefore only incomplete contracting can be achieved. (2) Also contracts are incomplete because agents may behave in an opportunistic way, more precisely may be dishonest and therefore confuse transactions. Consequently transactions are costly to define and monitor (Santos & Eisenhardt, 2005). While Williamson accounts the importance of human behavior and therefore departs from neoclassical economics critics claim that the two attributes of bounded rationality and opportunism are not enough to fully explain human behavior (Groenewegen, 1996). Ghoshal and Moran (1996) detail this criticism, by complaining that Williamson fails to distinguish between attitude and actual behavior of agents when it comes to opportunism. However, the relationship between attitude and behavior is important and a frequently discussed issue when it comes to human behavior (cf. Holland, Verplanken & van Knippenberg, 2002).

Behavioral theories

I take the criticism of TCE, that is, neglecting many aspects of human behavior (cf. (Groenewegen, 1996; Ghoshal & Moran, 1996) as a starting point to explore further theories that may contribute to sharpen the aspects of human behavior in the context of OCI communities. While bounded rationality and opportunism may explain while contracts are incomplete and costly to monitor, it does not answer further important questions, especially with regard to governance within OCI communities: Why do individuals contribute to communities without being paid (which may contradict with opportunistic behavior)? Why do agents behave non cooperative or free-ride (which can be classified as an opportunistic behavior)? Why do some governance structures receive more acceptances from the community? How is the process of designing governance mechanisms within a community? How are the effects of exogenous vs. endogenous governance on a community?

In an attempt to answer these questions resorting to concepts and theories rooted in social psychological research seems promising. One important aspect in social psychological research is the distinction between attitude and behavior. An important feature which TCE is lacking (cf. Ghoshal & Moran, 1996). Ajzen and Fishbein (1977) define what is to be understood by behavior and attitudes:

> "Attitudes are held with respect to some aspect of the individual's world, such as another person, a physical object, a behavior, or a policy."
> (Ajzen & Fishbein, 1977: 889)

Behaviors on the other hand are observable actions which are performed by an individual (Ajzen & Fishbein, 1977). A predictive relationship between attitude and behavior may seem intuitive. That is, that a certain attitude (e.g. positive attitude towards a politician) results in a certain behavior (in that case a vote for that candidate). However, research has shown that the relationship between attitudes and behavior is not as simple or universal. In a review of different studies relating attitude and behavior Wicker (1969) found, that attitudes are most likely unrelated or only slightly related to behavior. More recent research, comparing studies in a meta-analysis however disproves these findings and shows that attitudes are indeed related to behavior (Kraus, 1995). Maio and Haddock (2009) name two reasons for the inconsistency of these findings: First, attitudes measures have improved in contemporary research significantly which allows for a better prediction. Second, recent research applied better experimental paradigms, employing the needed accuracy when trying to predict behavior. Summarizing these findings, it can be said that indeed a relationship between attitudes and behavior exists. However, one has to approach the attitude-behavior relation with care. As it is not a simple one and is not universally valid, in the sense that attitudes not always predict behavior. The degree to which attitudes can predict behavior largely depends on the domain in question:

> "The question facing researchers is, therefore, no longer *whether* an individual's attitudes can be used to predict his overt behaviour, but *when*. The task is to specify those variables which determine whether an observed attitude-behavior relationship will be relatively strong or weak.
> (Regan & Fazio, 1977: 30)

Connecting these findings to my work it is important to identify attitudes which relate to the research object and may predict behavior of agents. More precisely, I have to identify attitudes of members in OCI communities which may influence their behavior. Since attitudes are directed towards an object (e.g. an attitude towards a specific person or the disposition towards church), it is important to define the objects in question.

Within this thesis I am interested in the effects of different governance schemes on the members of an OCI community. Therefore the first question is how attitudes of OCI members are towards the governance rules. When it comes to governance rules the question is not whether to have a positive or negative attitude towards the rules, but far more crucial is the question whether the governance rules are perceived as fair and legitimate. For a perception of legitimacy is crucial to the adherence of rules (Tyler, 2005). Therefore a perception of fairness of governance rules would represent an attitude towards the governance rules, which results in a certain behavior (in that case a higher compliance with the rule). Fairness can be measured via the construct of procedural justice (cf. Colquitt, 2001), which is embedded in the theory of procedural justice explaining under what circumstance governance rules are perceived as fair (cf. Solum, 2005). Procedural justice measures the perceived fairness of a procedural rule in a social system (Leventhal, 1980). Governance rules are closely linked to the person executing them (e.g. project leader). Therefore a second construct, namely interpersonal justice, is closely linked to the overall theory of justice. Interpersonal justice describes how a person perceives the execution of a rule by a decision maker, relating to aspects like respect and truthfulness (Bies & Shapiro, 1987).

The question of interpersonal behavior is closely linked to the second object, the attitude of individuals towards other community members. Due the collaborative aspects of OCI communities (see Chapter 2.2 and Chapter 4.3.1) members are working closely together. The interplay of group members inherits the risk of dissent and tension among community members. Research shows that too much conflict negatively impacts the performance of groups (de Dreu & Weingart, 2003). Therefore it is of interest, how a participant perceives the conflict within a community as it is likely to affect his behavior (e.g. by refusing to cooperate). Previous work on conflict within groups, especially groups handling innovative tasks, not only provides theoretical considerations but in addition proven constructs how to measure the perceived conflict within a group (cf. Amoson, 1996; Janssen, 2003; Wall & Nolan, 1986).

An often discussed question is what motivates volunteers to participate in OCI communities, particularly as they do not receive direct benefits at first sight. This contradicts with the self-interested-economic agent paradigm (Lerner & Tirole, 2001) and may also challenge the notion of opportunism of TCE. Consequently many authors have explored the question of participants' motivation within OCI communities (cf. Lakhani & von Hippel, 2003; Jeppesen & Frederiksen, 2006; Ghosh, 2005). Findings show that especially intrinsic motivation, that is, the enjoyment of the task itself is the strongest driving force within such communities (Lakhani & Wolf, 2005). Consequently my interest is focused on the intrinsic motivation of participants to perform the work within an OCI community.

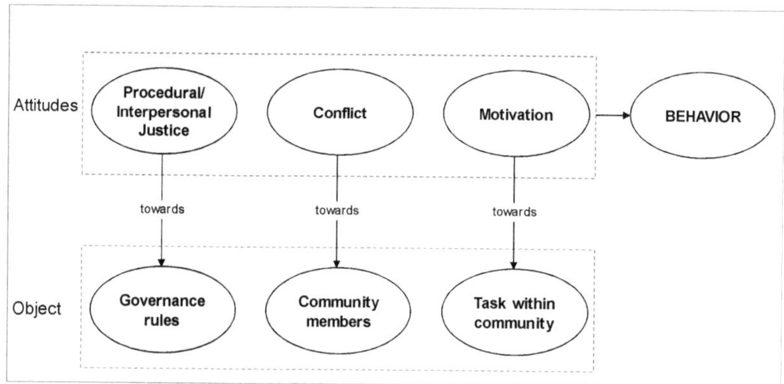

Figure 3: Perceived attitudes towards objects within the research setting

I believe that all different concepts, namely justice, conflict and motivation are strongly related to the behavior of individuals within OCI communities and therefore play a decisive role for a functional community (see Figure 3).

Introducing the concepts, I just briefly touched on them. Evidently much more detail is needed to adequately present the concepts and underlying theories. However, I do not describe them at that point of time. Within Chapter 4.1 I derive my research hypotheses resorting to these concepts, which includes a detailed review and classification of stated theories with regard to my research. Hence I do not want to anticipate the full presentation of these theories and concepts, but rather point to the mentioned chapter. Hence the previous paragraph was intended to briefly introduce the psychological concepts used within the thesis by linking them to TCE.

TCE in the context of OCI communities

Governance of OSS communities has been viewed through the lens of transaction costs. Demil and Lecocq (2006) compare the governance of such communities with the three modes defined by Williamson and conclude that a new form, namely bazaar governance is existent. Their conclusion for a new form of governance is based on the fact, that the governance in such communities is based on a new contract form (open license) and low intensity of incentive and control. To the contrary market governance is characterized by a classical contract, high incentives, low control, whereas hierarchy is characterized by employment contracts, low incentives and high control. To distinguish between bazaar and hybrid (or network) governance Demil and Lecocq point out that network governance is more closed and the personal ties are stronger.

Sidahmed and Gerlach (2009) apply the theory of governance, more specifically transaction cost economics (TCE) to OCI communities and their interaction with firms. They propose a new collaborative governance model, which is characterized by high level of information exchange, a higher level of flexibility, influence restraint limiting the power of different parties and shared responsibility.

While the work on economic governance, namely on TCE, by Williamson has gained some attention in the context of OCI communities my research is especially influenced by the work of Ostrom. For one reason because her Institutional Analysis and Development (IAD) framework has already proven to be applicable within the context of OCI communities, second it is a very helpful and well established framework to test hypotheses and propositions. Therefore Ostrom's IAD framework and her work on rules are described in more detail.

3.3 Institutional Analysis and Development (IAD) Framework

Understanding institutions is a key question of economic governance. The Institutional Analysis and Development (IAD) framework is an integrated composition of the work Ostrom's and different associates in their efforts to understand the functioning and development of such institutions. In her work Ostrom focused on institutions governing common-pool resources (CPRs). The original definition for a common-pool resource "[…] is a natural or man-made resource from which it is difficult to exclude or limit users once the resource is provided, and one person´s consumption of resource units makes those units unavailable to others." (Ostrom, 1999: 497). Classical examples include fish grounds or forests, however recently authors have extended this definition using the IAD framework to investigate the production of cultural commons such as open source software, *Wikipedia* or other knowledge resources (Madison et al., 2010). In her response to Madison et al. Ostrom herself highlighted the applicability of the IAD framework to this context (Ostrom, 2010). However, before discussing the application to the field of OCI communities the original framework shall be described properly.

A comprehensive description of the IAD framework and its elements can be found in Ostrom (2005). The framework consists of different elements. Furthermore the framework is characterized by a multi-level structure, meaning that elements on the highest level consist of further sub elements. This feature allows a researcher to zoom into a certain element to investigate it in more detail. On the highest level the framework consists of seven elements.

The central unit of the framework and analysis is the *Action Arena*, where two elements interact. Specifically *Participants*, who can be either individuals or corporate actors, interact within a given *Action Situation*. An *Action Situation* '[…] refers to the social space where participants with diverse preferences interact, exchange goods and services, solve problems, dominate one another, or fight […]" (Ostrom, 2005: 14). It is evident that such a definition includes nearly any interaction of an economic sense, more specifically production of goods and any buyer-seller exchange. The possible combinations of actors interacting are manifold as well, may it be a firm-firm, firm-individual or individual-individual interaction. The *Action Arena*, with its two elements, can be seen as a dependent variable which is influenced by a set of exogenous variables.

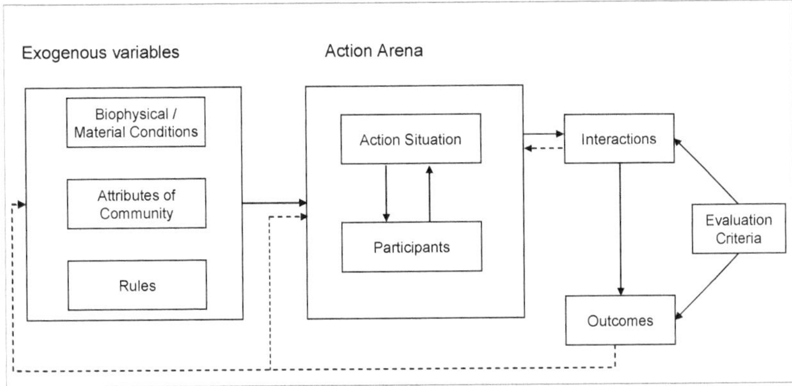

Figure 4: IAD Framework (Ostrom, 2005: 15)

An action situation is shaped by the *Biophysical and Material Conditions*, that is, "[w]hat actions are physical possible, what outcomes can be produced [...]" (Ostrom, 2005: 22). In practical terms this refers to goods or services produced or the technology available for the production. Linking this definition to the characteristics of OCI communities, two distinct features appear remarkable: First the special features of the goods produced (for example that for knowledge resources overuse is not a problem) and second the technology in form of the internet as the main communication device (see also Chapter 3.3.2. for a further discussion).

Another variable influencing the action situation are the *Attributes of Community*. Communities exist in many forms, with different extents of homogeneity, cultures and values. As already laid out in Chapter 2.2 even within the field of OCI communities many different communities exist, consisting of diverse members and producing different outcomes. The attributes of a community are therefore determined by the characteristics of its members and the interaction with each other. This may result in shared beliefs and norms, namely one specific community culture.

One of the most important variables influencing the action arena is *Rules*. Rules define what actions participants may or may not take. Since governance consists of a set of rules this variable is of particular importance within this dissertation project and is described in more detail within the next section.

On the other end of the action arena two more elements complete the framework. First *Interactions* of humans, that is, the actions they take and how they work together can be observed. From these interactions *Outcomes* result. Outcomes can be evaluated trough different criteria, such as economic efficiency, robustness of the behavior (e.g. how it changes over time), or equity (how benefits are distributed).

3.3.1 Focus on rules

Ostrom (2005) defines rules as "the syntax of a grammar of institutions" that need to be analyzed to understand such institutions. She gives two reasons, why to focus especially on rules. First, the impact of a rule change is a frequently asked question, second, adapting or designing rules to come to a preferable positive outcome is a more promising and stable approach than trying to influence the attributes of a community or the physical conditions.

To investigate the impact of different rules a syntax in order to describe rules is necessary. The syntax developed by Ostrom to describe rules consists of five components: (1) *Attribute* describing to whom the rules applies, for example a male or female. (2) *Deontic* as a holder of modal verbs such as 'may' or 'must'. (3) *Aim* is a holder for the action or outcome the deontic refers to. (4) *Conditions* is a holder that describes when an action or outcome is permitted or obligatory. (5) *Or Else* is a holder for the assigned consequences for non-compliance to the rule. Such an abstract syntax can be applied to all rules. Figure 5 shows an example of an application of Ostrom's syntax to a rule. It is important that not all elements of the syntax can always be explicitly identified for a rule. For instance, the example rule (see Figure 5) does not include a condition.

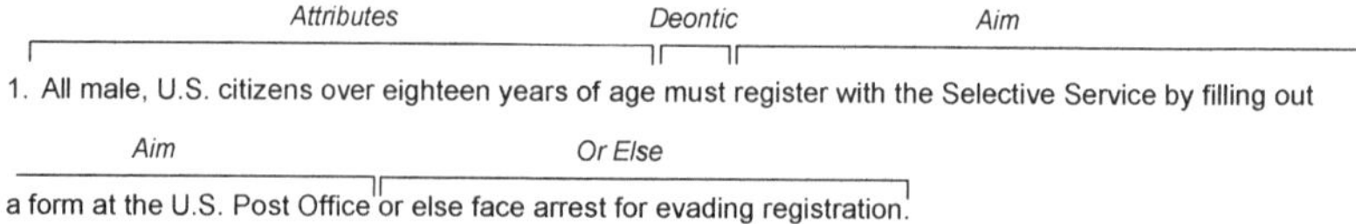

Figure 5: Example of key elements of rule syntax from Ostrom (2005); own representation

However, Ostrom states that even if no value for a condition is present, a default value applies. This means, that in the case of the example the rule applies at all times.

While Ostrom (2005) states that the general concept of rules in the IAD framework applies to explicit rules and implicit norms, the described syntax has an additional advantage. The different elements of the syntax allow for the description of all institutional statements, namely rules, norms and shared strategies. Rules consist of all components, norms just of the first four and shared strategies include only an *Attribute*, *Aim* and *Condition*. The distinction between these different types of institutional statements is especially important, considering that governance in many OCI communities consist of many informal norms (cf. Lerner & Tirole, 2002).

Besides the development of a syntax to describe rules a further contribution of Ostrom on the work of rules is the identification of seven generic rules. These seven generic rules are a result of extensive field research of Ostrom and her associates. As Ostrom states the development of generic rules is an attempt "[...] to cope with the immense diversity of rules by clustering them into seven generic rules." (Ostrom, 2005: 175). Ostrom identifies following rules: (1) *Position rules* describing positions of participants (e.g. project leader), (2) *Boundary rules* defining how to enter or exit a position (e.g. by vote), (3) *Choice rules* defining what a participant in a certain position must or must not do, (4) *Aggregation rules* determine whether decision are made by single or multiple participants, (5) *Information rules* define the channels and frequency of information as well as an official language, (6) *Payoff rules* describe what rewards or sanctions are assigned to specific outcomes or actions, (7) *Scope rules* focus on outcomes and link it with actions (e.g. basing promotions in the academic world on publishing records).

Evidence of the applicability of the classification framework within the context of OSS is provided by Schweik and Kitsing (2010) who matched the seven generic rules to concrete rules within an OSS community. The study reveals that all seven generic rules can be found within OSS communities. They furthermore provide a fine overview of the definition of the different rules as given by Ostrom (see Table 3).

To fully understand the classification framework it is important to point out that institutional arrangements are presented by a combination of different rules. An example given by Ostrom (2005) highlights this fact. In order to create a property right arrangement four rules need to be formulated, namely a position rule describing who owns the property, a boundary rule describing how to become an owner, choice rules describing the ability to exchange and aggregation rules regulating how exchanges are handled. This example gives an idea of the complex rule configuration even simple arrangements require. Nevertheless Ostrom's classification framework for rules and the IAD framework offer an excellent tool to investigate governance of communities as well as providing a theoretical base. It is therefore no surprise that different authors have made use of her work, applying it to the context of OCI communities.

Ostrom's Rule Category	Ostrom's Definition	Examples in OSGeo's[11] Institutional Design
Position Rules	Define the positions that participants hold	Board of Directors (BOD); President and CEO; Vice President; Committee Chair; Corporate Officer; Member; Participant
Boundary Rules	Define: (1) who is eligible to take a position (succession rules); (2) the process that determines which participants may enter (entry rules), such as by invitation, through some sort of competition, or compulsory; (3) how an individual can leave a position (exit rules). There may be also rules regarding the relationship between multiple positions, such as a mandate that no one person can hold multiple positions at the same time.	BOD election BOD member leaving Committee Chair Charter v. Other Members
Choice Rules	Specify what participants in positions must, must not or may do in their position and in particular circumstances. Choice rules focus on actions.	Bylaws for BOD; Bylaws for Officers Committee rules/policies Incubation process
Aggregation Rules	Determine whether a decision by a single or multiple participants is needed prior to an action at a decision point in a process. Aggregation rules are needed whenever choice rules provide multiple positions partial control over the same sort of actions. Aggregation rules can be symmetric (e.g., unanimity) or nonsymmetric (where a leader can make a decision for a group) and each also must include a non-agreement rule.	Symmetric: Consensus in Committees Nonsymmetric: BOD creates committees
Information Rules	Specify the channels used to communicate information among participants, as well as what kinds of information can be transmitted by what positions. There may also be rules specifying required frequency of interaction, or specifying an official language.	Required Meeting Minutes Required Meeting Notification Annual Meetings Required Financial Statements Required

---

[11] The Open Source Geospatial Foundation (OSGeo) supports open source projects working on geospatial technologies and was investigated in the study by Schweik and Kitsing (2010).

Payoff Rules	Assign external rewards or sanctions for particular actions or outcomes. For example, some payment for completion of a task.	Executive Director and others can be paid; BOD cannot be paid
Scope Rules	Specify which outcomes may, must, or must not be affected within a situation. Scope rules focus on outcomes (compared to choice rules which focus on actions).	Organizational Mission Committee Mission

Table 3: Ostrom's (2005) seven general rule categories matched to the rules within the OSGeo community (Schweik & Kitsing, 2010: 16)

3.3.2 Application of IAD framework in the context of OCI communities

The IAD framework and Ostrom's work on rules provide an excellent base for the study of OCI communities and therefore have been applied by different authors. However, the nature of communities producing innovative outcomes, mainly over the internet is different from managing conventional resources in a natural environment (e.g. fishers). A context the original IAD framework by Ostrom applies to. Therefore an adjustment to the context of OCI communities is necessary.

Ostrom's classification framework for generic rules has been successfully applied within the OSS context. Schweik and Kitsing (2010) showed that many of these rules exist in OSS communities (see also Table 3). The results of Schweik and Kitsing are based on one case study. However, further support for the finding that Ostrom's generic rules also apply to OCI communities can be found. In order to demonstrate this, I resort to the identified clusters of governance mechanisms, which are based on the work of multiple authors (see Table 2). Matching these clusters with the seven generic rules reveals a considerable degree of consistency. Many governance mechanisms correspond directly to one of Ostrom's generic rule, for example the communication cluster with information rules.

Governance Cluster / Ostrom's rules	Monitoring	Communication	Hierarchy & Roles	Decision rights	Property rights
Position Rules			X		X
Boundary Rules			X		X
Choice Rules				X	X
Aggregation Rules				X	
Information Rules		X			
Payoff Rules	X				X
Scope Rules	(X)				

Figure 6: Matched generic rules by Ostrom to identified governance mechanisms

However, Figure 6 shows that not always one-to-one assignments exist. Keeping in mind the complexity a simple property right requires (see Chapter 3.3.1), this is not surprising. Nevertheless the high consistency of Ostrom's generic rules with governance mechanisms in OCI communities gives further support that the framework is applicable within this context.

An application of the IAD framework has been carried out by Tenenberg (2008). Although he applies the framework not to an OCI community in the strict sense, but to a team of software developers, many parallels exist. As modern software teams work in a similar fashion to OSS projects and face the same collective action problems of unbalanced work and free-riding as OCI communities, many insights can be gained (cf. Tenenberg, 2008).

The most comprehensive and rigorous application as well as adaption of Ostrom's work within the context of OCI communities to date has been carried out by Madison et al. (2010). They shape the term "constructed cultural commons" in comparison to the classical natural common-pool resources (CPRs). According to their case studies, such cultural commons include patent pools, open source software, edited newspaper material and created musical pieces. This definition is congruent with all the different outcomes and types of OCI communities described in Chapter 2.2. Madison et al. (2010) point out three important features of such innovative cultural resources:

> "First, those who create, invent, innovate, and participate in similar intellectually driven, productive activities necessarily borrow from or share with others. It is impossible to divest oneself of that to which one has been exposed. Inevitably, the intellectual products of past and contemporary "producers" (a term that we use as a shorthand to refer to creators, inventors, innovators, thinkers, and the like) serve as inputs into each of our own productive activities. We necessarily borrow and share. Second, as discussed above, the resources that shape the cultural environment are by their nature naturally nonrivalrous and nonexcludable, meaning that knowledge resources are not naturally defined by boundaries that permit exclusion of users. Third, unlike resources in the natural world, resources of information and expression must be created before they can be shared. Because of the public goods character of these resources, a cultural commons must manage both use and production of cultural resources." (Madison et al., 2010: 672)

The distinct features of the cultural commons, that is, (1) the inevitability to base new work on the existing one, (2) the fact that cultural commons are nonrivalrous and cannot be overused and (3) that they do not exist per se, but must be produced first led to an adaption of the IAD framework. Comparing the framework with the original one, two major alterations exist. First, the features of the cultural commons require not only the governance of existing resources, but the production of those resources. Therefore the resources characteristics, attributes of the community and rules in use are much more "intertwined" (Madison et al., 2010). The produced resources, the community itself and the governance rules (rules-in-use) are highly dynamic. The value of knowledge resources (e.g. patents) can quickly perish. The same dynamics apply to the community members and the governance rules, as they are shaped by the community. Many different changing roles may exist, such as project leader or developer. Second, the separation of interaction and outcome does not account for the special features of cultural commons, therefore interactions are already an outcome in itself.

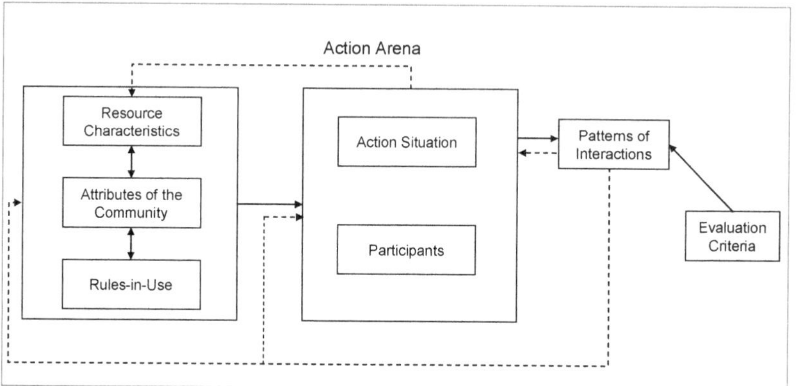

Figure 7: Adapted IAD framework for the cultural commons (Madison et al., 2010: 682)

A further important statement made by Madison et al. is the different role openness plays within the cultural commons. A classical community managing natural resources limits its openness to outsiders, since the finite character of natural resources would inventible lead to overuse. A community creating knowledge resources, such as an OCI community, does not face this risk since knowledge cannot be overused. However, such a community faces other challenges in their struggle to determine the right degree of openness. The authors differ between openness applied to resources and the openness of a community.[12] Openness of a resource "[...] describes the extent to which there are barriers to possession or use" (Madison et al., 2010: 695). In the concrete case of OCI communities this degree can be varied through the use of different types of licenses, granting or restricting the use of such resources. Openness applied to the community "[...] describes the extent to which there are criteria for or barriers to membership or participation in the creative or innovative processes [...]" (Madison et al., 2010: 696).

The degree of openness is represented through governance rules, that is, legal structures (e.g. intellectual property rights, licenses) and rules managing membership, sanctioning or distribution of information within the community. Assessing the openness of an OCI community is necessarily achieved by studying and assessing those governance mechanisms. However, since governance (rules-in-use) is dynamic

---

[12] A similar distinction is made by West and O'Mahony (2008) applying openness to intellectual property, governance and production within a community.

and inevitably 'intertwined' with the community itself, more precisely with the members of the community shaping and putting those rules in practice, one cannot study governance rules independent of the community. To fully understand, one has to put the process of how governance emerges and its effects on behavior of the community at the center of attention.

I try to contribute to an understanding with this dissertation thesis, by designing an experiment in order to investigate the effects of different degrees of openness of governance rules. The experiment contrasts one 'closed' model, with exogenous governance rules, giving a community no participation rights and an 'open' model, letting a community decide on their own governance rules.

4 RESEARCH DESIGN AND FRAMEWORK

The purpose of this chapter is to lay out the specific research questions and identify research hypotheses which can be tested. To achieve this, a research framework is used which is strongly based on the considered IAD framework of Ostrom. Whereas the IAD framework was theoretically explained in Chapter 3.3, the different units of it are now operationalized in order to design a laboratory experiment which imitates the phenomenon of open collaborative community innovation.[13] The aspiration for the framework is to provide a structure that allows for a systematic analysis by providing a clear definition of variables and their assumed relationships.

After detailing the research questions I give an overview of experiments as a research method and state the reason for choosing an experimental setup to answer the proposed question. I continue by explaining the research framework as a whole, then describing each element of the framework in more detail. By doing so I also present how the elements are operationalized and how variables are measured within the experimental setting, corresponding to prior work of different authors who have tested similar variables. After measurement of variables is established I finally formulate research hypotheses for the variables which are tested within the experimental study.

4.1 Detailed research questions – exogenous vs. self-governance

I have started my thesis raising the guiding question how a community of volunteers reacts to exogenous, firm initiated governance.

It has been stated that the question of governance is central within the firm-community relationship for different reasons. First, the conflicting goals of firm and

---

[13] As stated the used framework applied within the experimental study is strongly analogous with the IAD framework by Ostrom. However, in the context of this thesis the IAD framework is adopted to serve as a basis for the experimental study. Therefore *framework* and its described parts in this chapter evidently refer to the adopted framework. Even though most parts and terms of both frameworks are congruent, differences between certain aspects of the framework may exist. The reader should not mistake the adopted framework with the original one by Ostrom (which is extensively described and cited in Chapter 3.3).

community are likely to result in tension (West & O'Mahony, 2008). Second, the complexity is increased due a large number of parties with misaligned goals, different degrees of involvement and capabilities (Dahlander et al., 2008). Third, the finding that governance will influence the intrinsic motivation of participants to contribute (Jeppesen & Frederiksen, 2006) makes governance key to a flourishing community. This finding is in line with the discovery that volunteers show negative reactions if a firm executes too much control and unfair ownership demands (Shah, 2006). It has been already said that firms try to counter this problem through legitimization of the governance by letting the community participate, making the governance 'accessible' (West & O'Mahony, 2008). The uncertainty, whether such an approach is successful leads to my research questions. I take the guiding question raised at the beginning as a point of departure. To develop proper hypotheses which can be tested I formulate a more detailed research question, sharpening the guiding one. In order to measure the reaction of the group to exogenous governance, I investigate its effect on key factors, which I believe are important for a functional and thriving OCI community:

> *Research question 1 (R1):*
> *How does exogenous (firm-initiated) governance affect key factors of open collaborative innovation (OCI) communities compared to endogenous (community-initiated) governance?*

The so named key factors are conflict within the community, perceived justice, free-riding behavior and motivation of participants. The reason for choosing each factor is described in Chapter 4.3.2.

From this first research questions further sub-questions can be derived that seem worthwhile answering. The difficulty what enhances organizational performance has been studied in many contexts – a specific situation is the performance of an OCI community. Various research indicates that a relationship between the key factors (motivation, conflict, justice) and performance exist.[14] Therefore, the relationship between the identified key factors, behavior of participants and performance shall also be investigated:

---

[14] For a review of possible relationships and prior work see Chapter 4.3.2

Research question 2 (R2):
How are identified key factors and the behavior of participants and performance of the community related?

Furthermore, a set of research questions of more explorative nature shall be answered. One subject of great interest is the response and behavior of participants regarding the different modes of governance. While the first research question (R1) addresses specific key factors and investigates them on an individual level (individual members of a community) the following questions aim to identify aspects beyond these factors on a group level.

Research question 3 aims to identify how a group of volunteers handling an innovative task reacts to exogenous vs. endogenous rules at the exact point of time. The explorative nature of the question allows investigating additional factors which have been not taken into account.

Research question 3 (R3):
How does a community react to exogenously imposed governance rules compared to endogenously chosen rules?

In simple terms, the choice between different governance configurations can be classified into hierarchical and more grass-root democracy governance styles. A hierarchical style is characterized by a division of roles, where some roles are equipped with more power, namely decision rights over other roles. Contrary to that a grass-root style is characterized by an equal level of power among the group members. Within this context West and O'Mahony (2008) refer to the openness of governance, that is, the amount of decision-making control a community gives up. The ability of a group to select its own governance rules raises the question which choice they take – do they tend to a more grass-root style or the opposite, an hierarchical style, relinquishing decision power?

Research question 4 (R4):
Having the choice, does an OCI community prefer a more hierarchical over a grass-root democracy (open) governance style?

Even though governance rules play a vital role in the regulation of communities many implicit rules or norms exist that complement an explicit set of rules (Markus, 2007). Another reality is that communities develop different self-governing mechanisms.

Hence it shall be investigated what norms or rules the community creates beyond a given set of explicit governance rules:

> *Research question 5 (R5):*
> *What rules or norms does the community establish besides the given set of governance rules?*

4.2 Methodology: Experiment as a research method

I chose to answer these questions by conducting an experiment. First, this choice shall be properly justified. Furthermore, an overview over experimental methods and considerations when designing an experiment is given.

4.2.1 Experiment as the research method of choice

In order to answer the raised questions a number of research methods could be applied. There are several arguments that can be invoked for choosing an experiment. For one thing, the main research question is very suitable to be answered by an experiment. Exogenous vs. endogenous rules represent two extreme manifestations that can be easily implemented for an experimental manipulation. Secondly, an experiment is best fit for drawing conclusions about the cause and effect relationships between variables (Aronson, Wilson, & Akert, 2010; Colquitt, 2008). Since the research question aims at establishing such a cause-effect relationship between the mode of governance and key factors, an experiment seems best fit.

Another reason is that commonly applied methods in innovation research include mainly surveys and case studies (Sørensen, Mattsson, & Sundbo, 2010). While this statement refers to innovation research in general it is not less true for the research in the field of OCI communities. Applying a different research method to the same problem helps to gain broader insights. As Ostroms (2006) states:

> "One gains external validity in doing field research and internal validity in the laboratory. When a researcher can use both methods related to one theoretical set of questions, the scientific community can have more confidence in the results." (Ostrom, 2006: 150)

Sørensen et al (2010) also emphasize the lack of use of experimental methods in innovation research while highlighting the possible benefits of experiments:

"Thus, the experimental method distinguishes itself from traditional research methods applied in innovation research by having a clear focus on real life problem solving, and by following a direct path towards the creation and implementation of practically applicable knowledge, while simultaneously creating new and otherwise hardly retrievable scientific knowledge about innovation processes." (Sørensen et al., 2010: 319)

An additional advantage for the experimental setup is the possibility to collect a rich amount of data. This may be also true for field research. However, the laboratory environment allows assembling data from different sources to a particular extent.[15] The compilation of different sources and types of data permits the application of a multimethod approach, using both quantitative and qualitative methods. Such procedure is especially suitable when it comes to investigating complex group behavior, as shown by former authors:

"These methods permit me to investigate more thoroughly the sometimes elusive and sensitive aspects of group and organizational conflict." (Jehn, 1995: 257)

Therefore both methods are applied, first quantitative analysis in two separate studies supplemented by one qualitative study.

4.2.2 Different designs and criteria for high-quality experiments

When investigating the effect of one factor (one independent variable) generally a differentiation between *repeated measures design* and *between subjects design* can be made (Boniface, 1995). For the *repeated measures design* "[...] subjects are kept in a single group and each subject experiences all the conditions in a succession." (Boniface, 1995: 8). The *between-subject design* focuses on the comparison of subjects or groups under different conditions. When comparing these two designs one can also speak of *between-subject* comparison and *within-subjects comparison*.

Besides choosing the right experimental design a major objective is to reduce error as much as possible. One important fundamental is the *ceteris paribus* assumption, that all factors which might interfere with the investigated hypothesis are constant (Lüer & Becker, 1987). The adherence of this assumption is reached through rigorous control

---

[15] For example for the proposed experiment sources of data are self-reported measures of participants, as well as log files and recorded chat messages.

of such factors over treatments. Besides holding nuisance variables (variables which are an undesired source of variation) stable, Millsap and Maydeu-Olivares (2009) formulate two further approaches, which include assigning experimental groups randomly to the treatment to ensure that unsuspected sources of variation are distributed over the entire experiment and including nuisance variables as factors in the experiment.

All these requirements aim to reach internal validity, where "[...] the experiment has eliminated alternative causes of the phenomenon so that effects can be properly attributed to the variable under experimental control."(Willer & Walker, 2007: 39). Willer and Walker (2007) develop four maxims for well-designed empirical experiments which can be reached by applying the mentioned practices like random block design or inclusion of covariates. The four maxims are as follows:

" 1. Create at least two study conditions that are initially as identical as possible
2. Introduce a single difference between the two conditions and observe result.
3. Restrict all inferences about the result to the effect(s) of that single difference.
4. Infer relative regularities only if it is unlikely that they are due to chance."
(Willer & Walker, 2007: 39)

Yet one has to be aware that factors influencing the dependent variable unintentionally can be manifold. One example may be the behavior of the instructor or the instructions itself in course of an experiment. Such effects are a common issue for experiments and can be described as *framing effects*. Such effects come about "[ ] when different ways of describing the same choice problem change the choices that people make, even though the underlying information and choice options remain essentially the same." (Cookson, 2000: 55). While framing effects are to a certain degree inevitable, the researcher has to be well aware of the problem. He therefore must take great care when writing the instructions and also make an effort of keeping as much of the experimental instructions stable. In practice this would for example imply to refrain from giving improvised verbal instructions (even worse by different instructors with divergent styles of presenting) and rather record a standardized movie to instruct participants (in the case that written instructions are impracticable).

I describe how I implement these guidelines for good experiments in Chapter 5, presenting the detailed setup and procedure of the experiment.

4.3 Elements of the research framework

My research framework consists of five components. The *Action Arena* – as the term already suggests is the field where the actual work and interaction of participants around a given task happens. (1) *Action Situation*, in the case of this framework refers to the task the innovation community is working on – (2) *Participants* corresponds to the members of such a community. For the reason that the *Action Arena* is where actual activities are taking place it is the central area for analysis. Participants within the *Action Arena* are affected by exogenous variables, in the particular case by (3) *Governance Rules*. Not only can a distinction be made which rules exist, but whether such rules are imposed exogenously (e.g. by a firm) or endogenously by the participants themselves (by vote). *Governance Rules,* which affect the *Action Arena* lead to (4) *Interactions* that result in (5) *Outcomes. Interactions* can be seen as the actual activities and behavior by participants whereas *Outcomes* are the actual end results that allow the evaluation of overall performance. These *Interactions* and *Outcomes* in turn affect again the *Participants* and *Action Situation.*

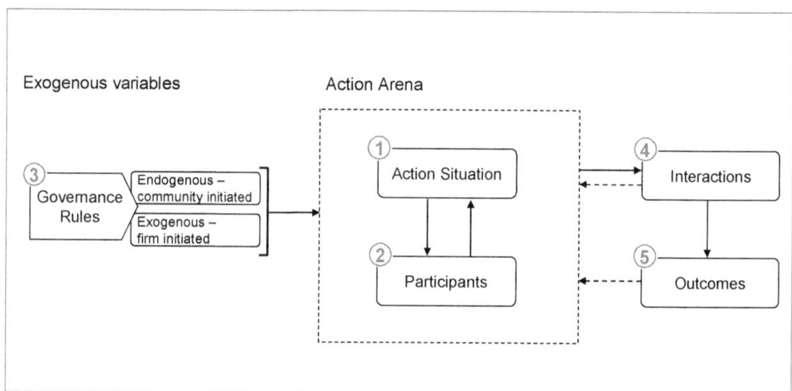

Figure 8: Research framework (adapted from Ostrom, 2005: 15)

4.3.1 Action Situation (1) – puzzle as a complex innovative task

One focal unit of analysis is the action situation. An action situation can be described as "[...] two or more individuals [...] faced with a set of potential actions that jointly produce outcomes [...]" (Ostrom, 2005: 32). Such action situations can be found within many contexts, for example buyer-seller exchanges, legislative processes and the creation of an innovative outcome in OCI communities.

Characteristics of innovative work in OCI communities

Before one can design an action situation that closely resembles a 'real life' OCI community, the characteristics of the work done within such communities have to be specified. According to Baldwin and von Hippel (2011) an open collaborative innovation project consists of contributors who share the work of generating a collective design. This indicates that a collective effort is an integral element of such communities. Raasch et al. (2009) highlight the collaborative aspect of several contributing actors. To allow for collaboration among many individuals, work in OCI communities is often described by modular design architecture (Baldwin & Clark, 2006). Such a system is characterized by elements that are partitioned into subsets and which can be processed separately (Baldwin & von Hippel, 2011). Furthermore, innovative work is differentiated by complexity (Katz & Tushman, 1979). This complexity is determined by many attributes, such as the option of multiple outcomes, multiple paths to reach the outcome, conflicting interdependence among paths and uncertainty about desired outcomes (Campbell, 1988).

In the light of these findings and characteristics of OCI communities (see Chapter 2.2) I define four features of tasks in OCI communities:

1. the solution must reflect a *collective effort* (one goal shared by the community)
2. it calls for *collaborative work* among actors
3. it shows features of *modularity*
4. it shows characteristics of *complexity* to resemble innovative work

A task, which is believed to reflect these requirements along with being feasible for an experimental setup is provided by Bavelas (1950) 'five square puzzle'. The puzzle consists of 15 various geometric shapes which are distributed among a group of five players. In order to succeed, each player must build an individual square by exchanging shapes with the other players. Out of these shapes many different squares can be formed, however there is only one arrangement, which allows every player to form his own square (see Figure 9).[16] The distribution at the beginning of the game increases the probability of suboptimal solutions, if those solutions are maintained a group solution remains impractical. It is notable how the group manages the occurrence of such 'wrong' squares, since "[f]or an individual who has completed a square, it is understandably difficult to tear it apart." (Bavelas, 1950: 730).

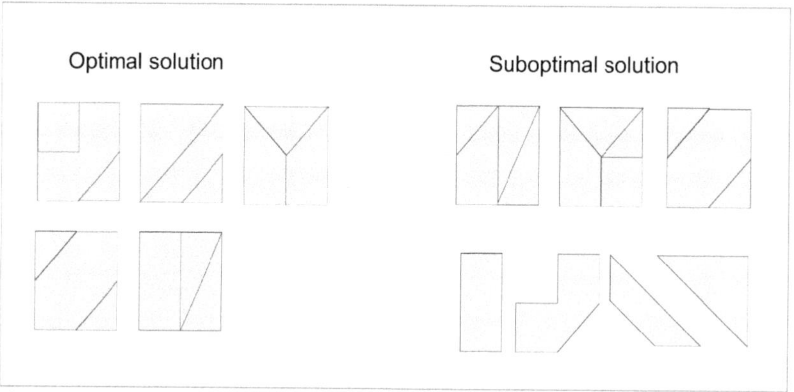

Figure 9: Optimal solution (left) and one of many suboptimal solutions of puzzle

Since a perfect solution can only be reached if everyone cooperates and trades pieces a (1) collective effort is needed. Trading pieces demands a high degree of mutual communication and interaction between participants – therefore (2) collaboration is inevitable. Furthermore, it shows some signs of (3) modularity since players can work

---

[16] Bavelas originally used this task to test communication structures. The five square puzzle recently has been used as team exercise.

on individual solutions (symbolized by individual squares). The described task clearly shows the feature of (4) complexity (Ruef, 1996), since different paths to the solution are possible.

While the chosen task meets the four established criteria some further features – that make the task even more suitable – shall be demonstrated. In order to solve the task, participants are faced with a social dilemma situation, where individual interest may conflict with the group interest (van Dijk & Wilke, 1995). A mixed motive situation may occur, if players who have already formed a square are faced with the decision to break up their solution, in order to contribute to the perfect solution. Such situation may quickly lead to free-riding behavior, in which case a player takes advantage of his position and refuses to cooperate (Torre, 2006), an often discussed problem in OCI communities (see Chapter 4.3.2.4).

The emergence of governance in OCI communities

While the puzzle game refers directly to the task a community is dealing with, further supporting processes exist within communities. One important aspect is the emergence of some form of governance. The type of governance can vary by its structure anywhere from implicit norms to a detailed structure. However, such a development usually starts with "[...] a process of cooperation without having to devise a full-blown organization with all of the rules that they might eventually need [...]" (Ostrom, 2000a: 149).

In order to allow for the evolution of governance part of the action situation provides participants an opportunity to have a group discussion prior to the actual puzzle task. Depending on two different treatments (exogenous vs. endogenous) these discussions are structured differently. The group under the first treatment is asked to decide on a set of presented governance rules (see Chapter 4.3.3 for an overview of presented rules) during the discussion. Such a situation is characterized as a typical example of group decision making. The choice a group eventually makes may be influenced by many factors, such as personal preferences and influential power of individuals (Corfman & Lehmann, 1987) as well as information about preferences and decision rules (Miller, 1985) and type of issue (Kaplan & Miller, 1987). Especially the decision rule, for instance whether a group comes to a verdict through majority or unanimity vote may influence the outcome and length a group requires to take a decision. However, findings are inconsistent with some studies showing that under unanimity decision rule decisions may take longer and groups even fail to come to a verdict (Miller, 1985) where other find no such effects (Kaplan & Miller, 1987). I am well aware of the possible effects of different decision modes. Nevertheless I implement no explicit decision rule. OCI communities are usually characterized by close to a grass-root democracy style without formal decision modes. Therefore, to resemble these characteristics best the group is just asked to agree on a set of rules. By imposing no formal rule on how to agree the decision rule itself remains an implicit variable, which is expected to have the least effect within the experimental study.

The second treatment group is given time to discuss any topic they like for a short period. Within this discussion external rules which are corresponding to the choice of the group under the first treatment are exogenously indoctrinated. The detailed setup and procedure is described in Chapter 5.

Contextual factors of the action situation

Additionally, another important feature concerns the environment in which a community operates. Coordination and aggregation of effort and products is done over the internet (Zwass, 2010). The effects of electronic communication on groups are often discussed, however, neither clear performance advantages or disadvantages (Kerr & Tindale, 2004) nor can consistent effects of the use of such technologies (Postmes, Spears, & Lea, 2000) be reported. Nevertheless, the virtual character of OCI community work shall be included when designing the experiment by transforming the physical puzzle game to a virtual environment.[17]

4.3.2 Participants (2) – Individual factors of participants

Participants who act in the action situation are the central unit of analysis within the framework. Ostrom specifies that "[w]ithout humans who make decisions in a situation, there is nothing but the biophysical world to explain." (Ostrom, 2005: 99). Participants'

---

[17] For a detailed description how the task is operationalized see Chapter 5.1.2.2.

behavior and actions are crucial to the success of an OCI community. In fact, they are the key factor for successful outcomes in a community.

I have discussed the relationship between attitude and behavior in Chapter 3.2. I also explained which attitudes are believed to influence the behavior of volunteers in OCI communities. It is known that motivation and cooperative behavior play an important role in maintaining functional collaborative communities (Bonaccorsi & Rossi, 2003). Therefore I examine key factors, namely motivation, justice, conflict, free-riding and interaction behavior of group members. The rationale for choosing each factor and the expected interrelations between the two modes of governance are illustrated in the following section.

4.3.2.1 Motivation

One of the key questions of OCI communities is why volunteers participate. This question is especially puzzling since the contribution to a public good is contrary to the "self-interested-economic-agent paradigm" (Lerner & Tirole, 2001).[18] Consequently, different authors investigate the motivation of users in such communities. Exploring the subject of motivation includes a wide range of different aspects for example the question why do users participate (cf. Lakhani & von Hippel, 2003) and why do they innovate (cf. Füller et al., 2007; Jeppesen & Frederiksen, 2006). Individuals vary substantially in their underlying motives (David & Shapiro, 2008). Ghosh points this out by showing the mix of different motives within a heterogenic group of participants:

> "Most models of FLOSS development assume one or another of these motives as the key driver. In fact, it turns out, the truth is all of the above, combined in different proportions for different people. [...] people don't always think consciously about their motives, and repetition and different phrasing help draw out more data and add perspective." (Ghosh, 2005: 26–27)

---

[18] While the theory of a rational, self-interested individual is widely accepted, studies show that individuals may behave contrary to this paradigm, calling for a broader theory of human behavior (Ostrom, 2000b).

In the attempt to organize such diverse motives, resorting to prior work in the field of motivation seems promising. Research on the topic of motivation typically makes a distinction between intrinsic and extrinsic types of motivation (Ryan & Deci, 2000). An activity is extrinsically motivated, if it is carried out in order to attain a certain extrinsic return – such as money or other rewards. Therefore, the source of the motivation "[...] comes not from the activity itself but rather from the extrinsic consequences to which the activity leads." (Gagné & Deci, 2005: 331). On the contrary, "[o]ne is said to be intrinsically motivated to perform an activity when he receives no apparent reward except the activity itself." (Deci, 1971: 105). The relationship between extrinsic and intrinsic motivation can be conflictive as substantial experimental and field evidence suggests (Bénabou & Tirole, 2003). In particular, an external reward that aims at enhancing external motivation may adversely affect intrinsic motivation. One such example of the conflictive nature is described by the motivation crowding effect where external intervention (such as monetary rewards or punishment) may undermine intrinsic motivation (cf. Frey & Jegen, 2000; Frey, 1994; Alexy & Leitner, 2010). In a meta-analysis Deci et al. (1999) showed, that there are various types of external influences going beyond just monetary rewards, ranging from verbal rewards to threats and deadlines, that conflict with intrinsic motivation. Frey and Jegen (2001) also formulate a general definition that all external intervention may affect intrinsic motivation, explicitly including regulations. Considering this research it is fair to say that the manipulation within the proposed study setup, by introducing exogenous vs. endogenous rules fits well within this range of external intervention affecting motivation.

With regards to OCI communities both intrinsic and extrinsic motivations have been identified. Features of intrinsic motivation include feelings, such as fun and a belonging to the group (Lakhani & von Hippel, 2003; Füller, 2006). Extrinsic motives consist of qualities, such as career prospects (Lakhani & von Hippel, 2003) and development of skills and knowledge, personal need and to some degree of monetary rewards (Füller, 2006).

While both intrinsic and extrinsic sources of motivation are important to understand community based innovation (Jeppesen & Molin, 2003), within this study I focus on intrinsic motivation. In the context of OSS communities there is evidence "[...] that enjoyment-based intrinsic motivation [...] is the strongest and most pervasive driver."

(Lakhani & Wolf, 2005: 3). Also the question whether external intervention by any form of authority (e.g. by firms) may mislay the interest and commitment of volunteers in OCI communities is raised (O'Mahony & Ferraro, 2007). Considering adjacent research from the field of motivation crowding theory and the work of Ostrom it seems to be worthwhile to investigate the relationship between external intervention and intrinsic motivation of participants. Ostrom showed that in some settings, when individuals lose a sense of control over their own fate external interventions crowds out intrinsic preferences (Ostrom, 2000b). Frey and Jegen (2001) identified two psychological processes by which external interventions can affect intrinsic motivation:

> "(a) Impaired self-determination. When individuals perceive an external intervention as reducing their self-determinination, intrinsic motivation is substituted by extrinsic control. [...]
> (b) Impaired self-esteem. When outside intervention carries the notion that the actor's motivation is not acknowledged, his or her intrinsic motivation is effectively rejected." (Frey & Jegen, 2001: 594)

Applying these findings to the stated problem I formulate following hypothesis:

HYPOTHESIS (H1): *Choosing your own governance rules has a positive effect on Motivation.*

Measurement

In a meta-analysis Cameron and Pierce (1994) showed that intrinsic motivation has been measured with a variety of means:

> "Intrinsic motivation has been measured as free time on task after withdrawal of reward; self-reports of task interest, satisfaction, and/or enjoyment; performance during the free time period (number of puzzles/problems solved, number of drawings completed, etc.); and subjects' willingness to participate in future projects without reward." (Cameron & Pierce, 1994: 374)

After a review of diverse measures, seven-point semantic differential scales developed by Crino and White (1982) are used to measure intrinsic motivation for two reasons:

	extremely	quite	slightly	neutral	slightly	quite	extremely	
monotonous	☐	☐	☐	☐	☐	☐	☐	exciting
ordinary	☐	☐	☐	☐	☐	☐	☐	novel
unenjoyable	☐	☐	☐	☐	☐	☐	☐	enjoyable
painful	☐	☐	☐	☐	☐	☐	☐	pleasurable
monotonous	☐	☐	☐	☐	☐	☐	☐	challenging
boring	☐	☐	☐	☐	☐	☐	☐	interesting
disappointing	☐	☐	☐	☐	☐	☐	☐	promising
frustrating	☐	☐	☐	☐	☐	☐	☐	gratifying

Table 4: Semantic differential scales used to measure intrinsic motivation by (Crino & White, 1982)

First, the task characteristics and setup by Crino and White is similar to the one in this research project (also a puzzle game, same group size). Second, and of less importance, measurement through a self-reported attitude scale can be integrated easily with measurement of the other variables via a questionnaire.

4.3.2.2 Procedural and Interpersonal Justice

Governance rules can solve problems of coordination and foster cooperative behavior among participants. However, rules can be only effective if they are being followed by participants. Therefore, research has focused on the circumstances required for individuals to comply with given rules. Models explaining individual rule compliance integrate factors from economic, psychological, and sociological theories (Jenny, Hechavarria Fuentes, & Mosler, 2007).

Being perceived as legitimate is in particular crucial to the adherence of rules (Tyler, 2005). Within the context of a governance system, legitimacy results in higher compliance of rules and therefore enduring stability (Walker, Thomas, & Zelditch,

1986). Thus, legitimacy is a prerequisite to build functional governance systems and therefore stable business institutions and OCI communities. This raises the question under what circumstances a normative rule system is perceived as legitimate. Put differently, how can one achieve legitimacy when designing governance rules and structures? One central dimension that influences the perception of legitimacy is justice (Tyler, 2006). Consequently, the construct of justice, especially in organizations has been of great interest to researchers within the last decades. Within the literature, justice is being viewed as multi-dimensional, differentiating between distributive justice, interpersonal justice and procedural justice. Distributive justice is fostered by outcomes and focuses on people's reaction to unfair allocation of rewards or resources (Greenberg, 1987).[19] Procedural justice centers the process by which the outcome is reached. Leventhal defines procedural justice as follows:

> "The concept of *procedural fairness* refers to an individual's perception of the fairness of procedural components of the social system that regulate the allocative process." (Leventhal, 1980: 35)[20]

Leventhal states that such a process includes complex networks of events and procedures such as the appointment of decision makers and the process of reaching decisions. Considering this definition it is evident that procedural justice directly applies to problem stated above – whether rules are perceived as legitimate or not. Since procedural justice focuses on the rules itself and not on interpersonal relationships or the outcome of rules it proves to be a precise measure to examine the effects of exogenous vs. endogenous governance rules. In addition the theory of procedural justice not only offers well-established constructs how to measure the perceived justice of governance rules, but also explains why endogenous rules are expected to be perceived as legitimate, because "[...] participation rights are essential for the legitimacy of adjudicatory procedures." (Solum, 2005: 179).

It is known that procedural justice is not only essential for the obedience of rules but also "[...] demonstrated to result in increased job satisfaction, organizational

---

[19] Given this definition distributive justice is not of great importance in my research setting, since I focus on governance rules and not the allocation of resources.

[20] Leventhal uses the term of procedural fairness rather than justice. However, the term justice and fairness within this context are used interchangeable (cf. Colquitt, 2001).

commitment, and organizational citizenship behaviors." (Konovsky, 2000: 492). Moreover, procedural justice is strongly related to individual innovative behavior (Janssen, 2004). One can therefore conclude that procedural justice is more than just a precondition for functional governance and indeed a lever to boost performance and innovation. Giving a group the opportunity to choose their own set of governance rules should lead to higher levels of perceived *Procedural Justice*, since participation rights (according to the procedural legitimacy thesis) increase the legitimacy.

HYPOTHESIS 2 (H2): *Choosing your own governance rules has a positive effect on the perception of Procedural Justice.*

Interpersonal justice, also referred to as interactional justice[21], is closely linked to procedural justice. Research shows that people not only focus on the fairness of the procedure but also how it is enacted by a decision maker, relating to dimensions such as truthfulness and respectful treatment (Bies & Shapiro, 1987). The close relationship between the procedure and the person endorsing it is intuitive. Various studies show high procedural-interactional justice correlations (Colquitt, 2001). It is important to distinguish between procedures that are perceived fair and the enactment of those rules. This is especially important when bearing in mind that rules are usually being executed by a person, for example by a project leader. The strong relationship between *Procedural* and *Interpersonal Justice* leads to the assumption, that the ability to choose your own rules also relates to higher levels of *Interpersonal Justice*. However, research of group decision processes shows that reaching a group decision may be a delicate issue, potentially resulting in conflict and poor decision quality (cf. Priem & Harrison, 1995). Green highlights the negative effects a group decision can have on socio-emotional behavior by investigating different social decision schemes within groups (Green & Taber, 1980):[22]

---

[21] Colquitt (2001) uses the term interpersonal justice however refers to the original work of other authors who apply the term of interactional justice. Since the used items are based on Colquitt the term interpersonal justice is used within this thesis.

[22] Socio-emotional as Green uses it refers to behaviour of others within in the process and therefore shows great overlaps with the construct of *Interpersonal Justice*.

"There are costs, however, in providing for such involvement. While the consensus and majority vote schemes produced greater feelings of personal participation, they also contributed to higher amounts of negative socio-emotional behaviors than did the nominal voting scheme." (Green & Taber, 1980: 104–105)

Depending on whether the group comes to an easy verdict or finds itself in a difficult discussion in the process of agreeing on rules, different effects on the dimension of *Interpersonal Justice* are expected. Overall, justice is an important factor when it comes to endogenous vs. exogenous rules. However, I did not have an a priori hypothesis of the directional effect.

HYPOTHESIS 3 (H3): *Choosing your own governance rules has an effect on the perception of Interpersonal Justice.*

Measurement

Various measurements for the dimensions of *Procedural* and *Interpersonal Justice* exist (for an overview and a validation of different measures see Colquitt (2001)).

Variable & Measure Item	Source on which item is based on
Procedural Justice	
Have you been able to express your views and feelings during those actions?	(Colquitt, 2001)
Have you had influence over the (outcome) arrived at by those actions?	(Colquitt, 2001)
Have those rules been applied consistently?	(Colquitt, 2001)
Have those rules been free of bias?	(Colquitt, 2001)
Interpersonal Justice	
Have they treated you in a polite manner?	(Colquitt, 2001)
Have they treated you with dignity?	(Colquitt, 2001)
Have they treated you with respect?	(Colquitt, 2001)
Have they refrained from improper remarks or comments?	(Colquitt, 2001)

Table 5: Items and source for measuring dimensions of justice[23]

---

[23] Items were slightly adapted to the context e.g. replacing the word "procedures" by "rules" and referring to the game as a specific situation.

Drawing on the work of Colquitt, well established items are used to measure the two variables *Procedural Justice* and *Interpersonal Justice*. Both variables are measured on a 5-point scale with anchors of 1 = *not at all* and 5 = *to an exceptional degree*.

4.3.2.3 Conflict

Faced with an innovative and complex task, groups experience problems of optimal coordination and communication which results in conflict, a struggle which governance mechanisms may help to solve (Lattemann & Stieglitz, 2005). Especially innovative behavior of individuals may provoke conflict with co-workers, if innovative ideas challenge the established framework of collaborators (Janssen, 2003). Innovative tasks are therefore more likely to breed conflict for two reasons: First, problems of coordination and second, different intensity of innovative behavior of individuals. To some level conflict can be beneficial by generating new ideas, however, too much conflict becomes dysfunctional (Wall & Nolan, 1986). In more detail, two studies showed that innovation increases with a medium level of conflict within a team, while dropping to zero under intense conflict (de Dreu, 2006) (see Figure 10).

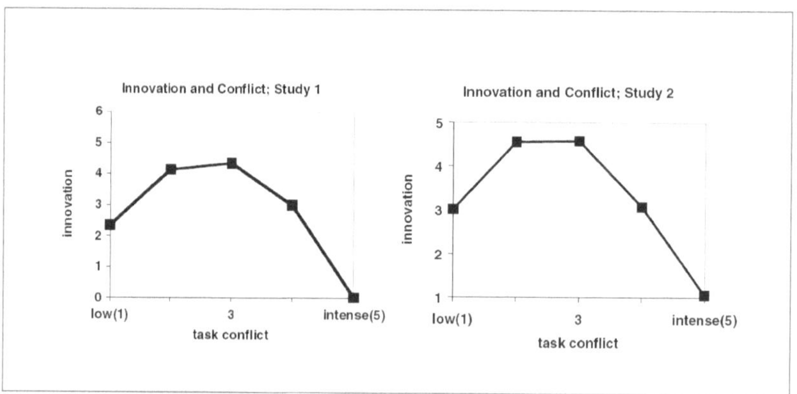

Figure 10: Curvilinear relationship between task conflict and team innovation (de Dreu, 2006: 92, 99)

Not only the level of conflict is decisive, but also the type of conflict. Conflict is distinguished between two forms – task oriented and interpersonal conflict (cf. Jehn, 1995). Amason's (1996) distinction between functional cognitive conflict and affective conflict is in line with this classification. Affective conflict is characterized by personal incompatibilities or disputes and tends to be emotional, where cognitive conflict is task-oriented and encourages evaluations of alternatives. Therefore, cognitive conflict is expected to contribute to innovation, while affective conflict may demolish innovative outcomes.

In the light of the negative consequences too much conflict can have, the matter of managing conflict within communities needs to be solved. Hence, effective and good governance must hinder the emergence of too much conflict and solve it rapidly when inevitable. Kittur and Kraut (2010) found procedures and policy likely to be the only coordination devices to be effective:

> "The only coordination mechanism we studied that had a significant main effect of reducing conflict was policy and procedural work. On the one hand it appears that active policies and procedures can have a direct influence on managing conflict. However, this was also the only coordination mechanism that had a positive interaction with the number of editors, indicating that as wikis accumulate more editors, changes to their policies and procedures are associated with greater conflict in subsequent time periods." (Kittur & Kraut, 2010: 222)

Such procedures and policies are consistent with the governance rules discussed in Chapter 4.3.3 which affect the participants within the action arena. Since I propose that rules selected by the community may have higher perceived legitimacy (hypothesis H2) it could be expected that self-chosen rules reduce conflict better. However, the positive effect of procedures and policies can only be attained if such rules are in place. The process of agreeing on rules, as mentioned before, involves the risk of creating further conflict. Therefore, once again hypotheses are formulated non-directional, as for *Interpersonal Justice*:

HYPOTHESIS (H4): *Choosing your own governance rules has an effect on Affective Conflict.*

HYPOTHESIS (H5): *Choosing your own governance rules has an effect on Cognitive Conflict.*

Measurement

Accommodating for multidimensional aspect of conflict I measure dysfunctional and functional conflict with two constructs. I draw on the work of Amason, who distinguished between dysfunctional *Affective Conflict* and functional *Cognitive Conflict* (Amason, 1996). *Cognitive* and *Affective Conflict* are measured using seven items from a scale used by Amason (1996)[24] applying a five-point, Likert-type scale with anchors of 1 = *not at all* and 5 = *to an exceptional degree*.

Variable & Measure Item	Source on which item is based on
Affective Conflict	
How much anger was there among the group during the game?	(Amason, 1996)
How much personal friction was there in the group during the game?	(Amason, 1996)
How much were personality clashes between group members evident during the game?	(Amason, 1996)
How much tension was there in the group during the game?	(Amason, 1996)
Cognitive Conflict	
How many disagreements over different ideas about decisions and actions were there?	(Amason, 1996)
How many differences about the content of decisions and actions did the group have to work through?	(Amason, 1996)
How many differences of opinion were there within the group over actions and decisions?	(Amason, 1996)

Table 6: Items and source for measuring conflict[25]

---

[24] The scale was originally developed by Jehn (1995).

[25] Items were slightly adapted to the context for example replacing the word 'situation' with 'game'.

4.3.2.4 Free-riding and cooperation

One of the great challenges of open source communities is to prevent free-riding and sustain cooperation (Bonaccorsi & Rossi, 2003). The free-riding assumption is a commonly discussed problem when it comes to the production of public goods, when "[...] agents, acting in their own self-interest, will under reveal demand, thus leading to a suboptimal allocation of resources to the public good." (Isacc & Walker, 1988: 585). While free-riding in the classical sense often relates to the mentioned suboptimal allocation or the overuse of resources, free-riding in the context of open collaborative innovation shows some different features. The resource produced and shared in OCI communities in a broader sense is knowledge – may it be source code or design specifications. Knowledge, however, cannot be overused. Madison et al. point out the special characteristics of knowledge within such communities:

> "The cumulative and aggregative character of knowledge is fundamental to human culture. Producers of knowledge and culture resources are therefore simultaneously users and consumers." (Madison et al., 2010: 697)

Therefore, functional OCI communities have to ensure the balance between consumption and production. Free-riding in OCI communities may be consequently characterized as pure consumption of work of others, a behavior which is likely to occur "[b]ecause contributions to a collective action project are a public good, potential beneficiaries of that good have the option of waiting for others to contribute and then free-riding on what they have done."(von Hippel & von Krogh, 2003: 213). Such behavior of non-contribution and pure consumption has been identified within virtual communities (cf. Kannan, Chang, & Whinston, 2000; Kollock & Smith, 1996), a behavior which Nonneke and Preece (2000) portray as „lurking" – a manner which according to their study reflects the majority of virtual communities.

Given the nature and structure of the puzzle game it is expected that free-riding takes place when participants refuse to break up their individual solution, hindering the group to achieve the perfect solution – a typical action of free-riding where some players "[...] take advantage of their position to escape from their commitments in terms of quality or appropriate a major part of the rent." (Torre, 2006: 65). Governance rules may solve such problems. In the context of the proposed study the decision rights for exchanging pieces (see Chapter 4.3.3) could mitigate the problem of free-riding in particular. Since the endogenous rules are expected to reach higher levels of legitimacy and acceptance (see Chapter 4.3.2.2) less free-riding is expected if a group chooses its own rules:

HYPOTHESIS (H6): *Choosing your own governance rules has a positive effect on Free-riding (less Free-riding).*

Measurement

A prominent measure for *Free-riding* is asking group members to mutually evaluate each other by distributing a certain amount of points among their group (cf. (Tenenberg, 2008; Brooks & Ammons, 2003). Consequently, the established scale used by Tenenberg is applied in order to measure *Free-riding* by asking participants at the end of the game:

> *Suppose you have 40 units of something desirable to distribute across your team in proportion to their overall contribution, cooperation and effort during this game. Please distribute the units accordingly.*

4.3.3 Governance rules (3) – rules from the inside vs. from the outside

Different exogenous variables act upon the *Action Arena* (see Chapter 3.3) and influence participants in the given *Action Situation*. Within this thesis, the influence of governance rules is of special interest. Governance rules therefore function as the independent variable, which is expected to affect the dependent variables, represented by the key factors of participants (see Chapter 4.3.2). Given the main research question the concern is not the consequence of different governance rules on participants, but the consequence of whether a group is able to choose their own rules or has to follow exogenously imposed rules. Therefore, the independent variable is manipulated to reveal two conditions, namely treatment $A_{end.}$ with endogenous chosen rules and treatment $B_{exog.}$ with exogenous imposed rules.

Before the aspired manipulation is carried out a set of governance rules has to be developed. Such rules have to be specific to the action situation. Governance rules within the context of the game should accomplish two principles: First, resemble governance rules used in real life OCI communities and second help the group perform better by addressing issues, such as conflict and enhancing cooperation behavior of individuals (see Chapter 4.3.2). In order to achieve this objective, a list of rules resting on research on governance rules of existing communities (see Chapter 2.2.1; 3.3.2) was developed and tested during pre-tests.[26] Such tests resulted in two blocks of rules from which participants are able to choose under treatment $A_{end.}$. The first block provides participants with the option to have a project leader. Roles like the one of project leader are frequently found in OCI projects (cf. von Hippel & von Krogh, 2003; Lerner & Tirole, 2002; O'Mahony & Ferraro, 2007).

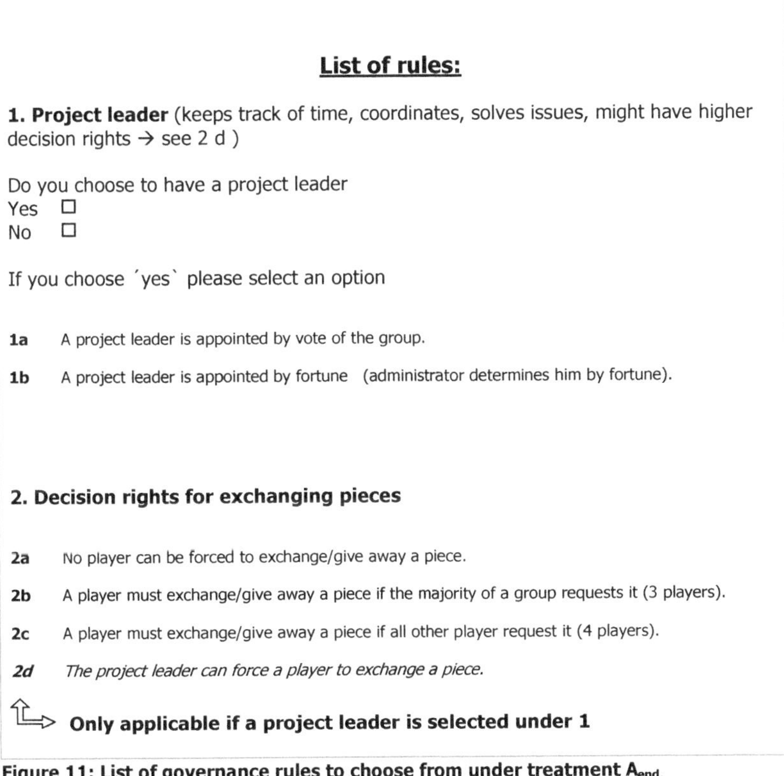

Figure 11: List of governance rules to choose from under treatment $A_{end.}$

---

[26] For detailed description how pre-tests were conducted see chapter 5.1.2.1

Depending on the community, project leader tasks as well as the process of appointment differ. Within the proposed experiment participants could – once they decided to have a project leader – choose between two options:

1. Having a group vote to determine a project leader
2. Appointing the project leader by fortune

The second block is concerned with different decision rights when it comes to sharing puzzle pieces. While these rules specifically apply to the puzzle task similar rules, for example decision rights over releasing code and solving conflicts are found in OSS communities (cf. Shah, 2006; Markus, 2007). Again, the group can choose between different options. One alternative is transferring all the decision power about breaking up squares to the project leader. Another two choices are installing different decision schemes where a simple majority of three or an exhaustive majority of four has to agree. The last option implies leaving all decision right with each individual. Figure 11 gives an overview of the different rules to choose from as they were presented during the experiment.

4.3.4 Interactions (4) – behavior resulting from the action arena

While key factors described in the previous chapter express the self-reported view of each individual another unit of analysis is the behavior and resulting interaction between participants. Interactions provide a further measure to balance subjective and objective observations. Both types of variables, individual self-reported factors of participants and the interactions variables are related, because the self-reported factors are antecedent of human behavior. Specific behavior results from motivational processes, which are affected by individual inputs (e.g. ability, knowledge, believes) and context (e.g. task design, rewards, social norms) (Mitchel & Daniels, 2003). The directional aspect between those factors and the consequential behavior, resulting in performance is evident. Two different measures are introduced to evaluate interactions.

A frequently used analysis is measurement of activity or participation within the community by counting email messages (cf. Dahlander & Wallin, 2006) or code contributions (cf. Roberts et al., 2006). A reason for this is that activity, expressed by contributions of members, is a good indicator for the success of a community. Only a critical mass of participation lets a community thrive (Bonaccorsi & Rossi, 2003). Dahlander et al. (2008) point out the importance of communication, highlighting that it is much more than a proliferation device but the key mechanism to produce creative and valuable outcome.

Two distinct variables are introduced to capture participation. First, $Messages_{sent}$ modeled by the total number of messages a player sends during the game. This variable is akin to the described measure of email messages or posts in 'real-life' communities. If groups are able to reach a perfect solution, they may finish the task prior to the given time frame. Consequently, $Messages_{sent}$ is standardized by the group time needed, resulting in messages sent per minute for each player during the game:

$$Messages_{sent} = \Sigma\ Messages\ /\ Group\ Time$$

However, investigating communication behavior of participants is just one element for an active community. One could argue that 'talk is cheap' and pure frequency of communication is not an indicator of a capable community.[27] Therefore, another variable is introduced – $Pieces_{sent}$ measuring the pieces send between the participants. Rather than the sole frequency of messages, this variable gives an indication how much a participant contributed to the solution and whether he behaved cooperatively.[28] Unlike the variable $Messages_{sent}$ the total number of pieces sent is not strongly related to the time a group takes to come to a solution.[29] Therefore $Pieces_{sent}$ is not standardized by group time. However, the pure number of puzzle pieces send in course of the game does not take into account that pieces are often traded in return for another piece. Therefore, a player may send many pieces but still receive an even larger number. To clear this unwanted effect the sum of pieces send is divided by sum of pieces received:

$$Pieces_{sent} = \Sigma\ Pieces\ sent\ /\ \Sigma\ Pieces\ received$$

---

[27] Obviously statistical analysis requires quantitative measures, such as number of messages. For qualitative insights on the content of the communication see study 3.

A participant who has a value higher than 1 would therefore have sent more pieces than he has received, a value below 1 would indicate a higher number of received pieces whereas 1 would account for a balance of sent and received pieces.

To investigate the association between the self-reported factors (*Motivation, Justice, Conflict*) and *Messages$_{sent}$* and *Pieces$_{sent}$*, a second set of hypotheses is formulated. Hypotheses for both variables can easily be derived from the already presented argumentation and prior research. Since hypotheses for both variables point into the same direction, they are presented in one block.

Findings from motivation research suggest that higher motivation is reflected by more participation (Roberts et al., 2006) which is likely to result in a higher amount of messages and send pieces by players, reflected in following hypotheses:

HYPOTHESIS (H7): *Participants Motivation is positively related to the number of Messages$_{sent}$.*

HYPOTHESIS (H8): *Participants Motivation is positively related to number of Pieces$_{sent}$.*

Trying to formulate hypotheses relating the number of messages sent and the level of conflict is complicated. One possibility is that conflict leads to frustration causing a retreat from the community which would reduce the frequency of communication. Another possibility is that conflict leads to an increase in the number of messages, since the intensity of communication increases. Since no reasonable relationship can be derived the formulation of a hypothesis is delayed. Considering the other variable *Pieces$_{sent}$*, a relationship seems recognizable. The higher the level of conflict the more likely a participant refuses to share his pieces:

HYPOTHESIS (H9): *Affective Conflict is negatively related to the number of Pieces$_{sent}$.*

HYPOTHESIS (H10): *Cognitive Conflict is negatively related to number of Pieces$_{sent}$.*

---

[28] This variable is akin to the mentioned code contribution of participants.

[29] Depending on a chosen strategy of a group players could rapidly exchange pieces, or choose to first explain pieces carefully. This would result in fewer pieces sent. So the total number of pieces exchanged during a game is more linked to the chosen strategy than to the time played.

The same reason may apply to justice. While the existence of a relationship between justice and the number of messages seems unlikely, the perception of justice may positively influence the number of pieces sent.

HYPOTHESIS (H11): *Procedural Justice is positively related to the number of Pieces$_{sent}$.*

HYPOTHESIS (H12): *Interpersonal Justice is positively related to the number of Pieces$_{sent}$.*

4.3.5 Outcomes (5) – measuring the overall performance

While a result of psychological states such as motivation is a certain behavior, performance emerging from such behavior is described as "[...] an outside standard that is determined by the organization and usually assessed by others." (Mitchel & Daniels, 2003: 227). In the case of OCI communities performance measures could be manifold, either relating to the individual contribution of members (Roberts et al., 2006) or to the overall solution, investigating its functionality and creativity (Lerner & Tirole, 2002). For the given task in the experimental setup, performance is measured by focusing on the outcome. Since individuals are rewarded by points for their personal and group performance (based on how many squares they were able to form) each individual receives a certain number of points.[30] Another implicit variable of performance is the time the group takes to reach the outcome. Therefore, *Performance* is measured as follows:

Performance = Individual Points / Group Time

Prior research has related motivation positively to task performance (Roberts et al., 2006). This is true for both individuals and groups (Shepperd, 1993). Hence, a positive relationship between motivation and performance is expected:

HYPOTHESIS (H13): *Motivation is positively related to the Performance of participants.*

---

[30] For a detailed description of point allocation see Chapter 5.1.1

The relationship between conflict and performance of groups and organizations has been subject to substantial research, however "[...] no integrated theory of the benefits and detriments of conflict currently exists" (Jehn, 1995: 256). Some findings suggest that the absence of conflict is related to higher performance (Gladstein, 1984) and satisfaction (Wall & Nolan, 1986) while other findings suggest that conflict improves the quality of decisions (Schweiger, Sandberg, & Ragan, 1986) and leads to higher growth rates of firms (Eisenhardt & Schoonhoven, 1990). While the distinction between conflict related to task issues and interpersonal relationships is widely used (see Chapter 4.3.2.3) the relationship of both types of conflict with performance is ambiguous. Jehn (1995), for example, argues that task conflict is positively related to team performance. However, Dreu and Weingart (2003) show in a meta-analysis of the association between relationship conflict, task conflict and team performance, that "[...] the idea that task and relationship conflict have different consequences for team performance." (de Dreu & Weingart, 2003: 745) cannot be verified. They rather show that for both types of conflict a negative relationship between conflict and performance exist. Hence, I formulate following hypotheses:

HYPOTHESIS (H14): *Affective Conflict is negatively related to the Performance of participants.*

HYPOTHESIS (H15): *Cognitive Conflict is negatively related to the Performance of participants.*

Justice is positively associated with organizational citizenship behavior (Konovsky, 2000: 492; Chiaburu, 2007) (see also Chapter 4.3.2.2). Furthermore, it is known that citizenship behavior is likely to result in higher levels of performance (Podsakoff, Ahearne, & MacKenzie, 1997). Therefore, I expect both measures for justice to be positively related to *Performance*:

HYPOTHESIS (H16): *Procedural Justice is positively related to the Performance of participants.*

HYPOTHESIS (H17): *Interpersonal Justice is positively related to the Performance of participants.*

5 EMPIRICAL STUDY

The previous chapter laid the foundations for the empirical study by explaining the methodological approach, describing different variables and estimating their relationships. This chapter deals with the detailed setup of the experiment. More precisely, this includes the exact design and procedure for the experiment, the experimental setup and the sampling of subjects.

5.1 Experimental design and procedure

The choice for a between subject design for the proposed experiment is unambiguous, considering the described features of the puzzle task. Letting teams play the game repeatedly would definitely lead to practice effects where players get familiar with the game design.

In order to control for other factors, a randomized block design is chosen, where players are randomly assigned to the different treatments. Since participants for the experimental sessions are all from one relatively homogeneous sample (students from one course of studies), they are expected to have similar values for possible influential factors such as intelligence, skills, education and attitudes. However, certain control variables (e.g. native language, typing speed) are recorded to include them into the statistical analysis (see Chapter 5.1.2.4.) Also, different precautionary measures are taken to rule out framing effects (see Chapter 5.1.4) or other distracting factors as much as possible. The detailed setup and procedure for the experiment are described in the following section.

5.1.1 Basic Design

The fundamental design is based on the *five squares puzzle* by Bavelas (1950) which has already been introduced and discussed in Chapter 4.3.1. The initial distribution of pieces is arranged according to Bavelas (1950) original design to make false or not perfect solutions more likely (see Figure 12).

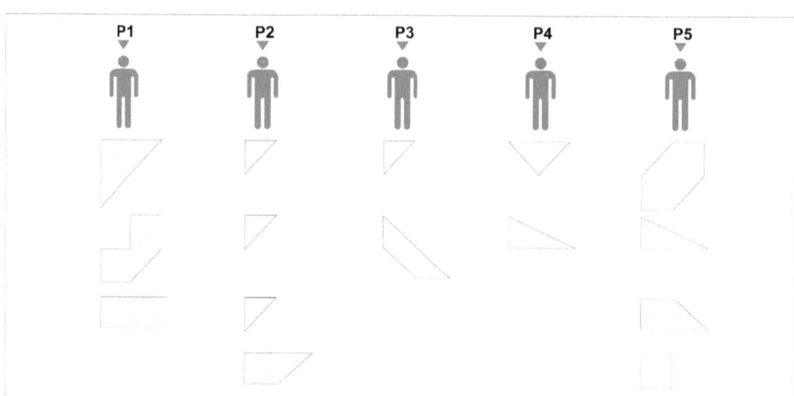

Figure 12: Allocation of pieces at the beginning of the game

Players are given 40 minutes to solve the task. To increase the already in the game characteristics inherent social dilemma – when players are faced with the decision to break up a suboptimal square – a payoff function is introduced. Players are awarded with points, whereas the point allocation is determined by the individual and group performance. After the game is finished a count of completed squares for each group is carried out. Points for each player are calculated by following formula:

$$\textit{20 points for individual square} + \Sigma \textit{ group squares x 10}$$

Hence a player could reach 0-70 points depending on both the individual and group performance (see payoff table, Figure 13, unterhalb for possible point allocations. To provide an incentive the 5 players with the highest number of points (across all teams) are awarded with a voucher worth 20 €. If there were more than 5 participants with the same number of points, the group time needed to reach the solution was taken into account as an additional criterion.

Before the actual game start participants engage in 15 minutes long group discussions. Topic and purpose of the group discussion vary among both treatments, as described in the following chapter.

Number of total **group squares** formed						
	0	*1*	*2*	*3*	*4*	*5*
Own square	N/A	30	40	50	60	70
No own square	0	10	20	30	40	N/A

Figure 13: Payoff table of points for different possible solutions

5.1.2 Pre-tests, experimental setup and sampling of subjects

5.1.2.1 Pre-tests

While designing the experiment, four pre-tests were conducted. Main goals of these pre-tests were to (1) to develop a specific set of governance rules, (2) find an ideal payoff function to create the desired *social dilemma* and (3) assure comprehensibleness of the game instructions and usability of the tool. The first two pre-tests were conducted in a non-virtual setting since the software tool was not yet available. After having played the game players were asked what rules might have helped them perform better.[31] Furthermore, the effect of the given payoff function was examined, which led to a raise of the amount of points a player would get for his individual square. The last two pre-tests were carried out in a virtual setting both under treatment $A_{end.}$ – endogenous governance rules. Findings from these two tests resulted mainly in adaption of the instructions. Further, the set of rules to choose from was reduced from three blocks of rules to two – since the possible configurations of three blocks of rules showed to be too complex.[32] Another focus of pre-testing was to adjust the timing for the different phases within the experiment – especially time needed for the group discussion and to solve the game. From the four groups playing

---

[31] Out of these findings and results from prior research a set of rules for the manipulation was created (see Chapter 4.3.3).

[32] Even with two blocks of rules 11 different configurations are possible.

the game, two were able to come to a perfect solution with an average time of 35 minutes. Two groups did not come to a perfect solution within the given timeframe of 40 minutes.

Further findings from the pre-tests showed that expected effects of group behavior such as conflict within the group and free-riding (unwillingness to share/exchange pieces) behavior occurred in the experimental setting.

5.1.2.2 Experimental setup and software application

Players were seated in one room in front of computer terminals, which were divided by blinds. The administrator was located in the same room during the whole experiment (see Figure 14).

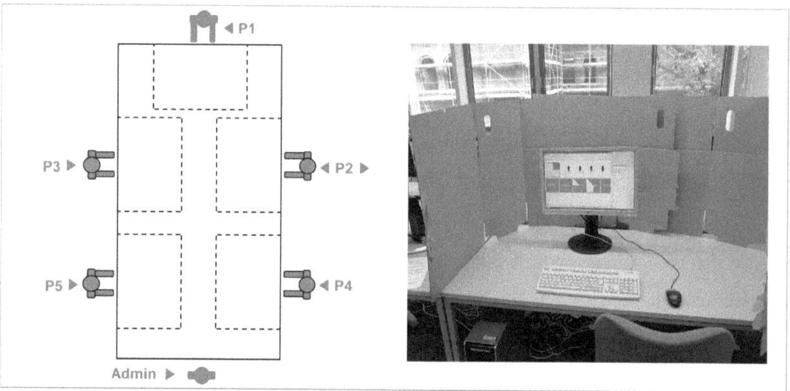

Figure 14: Seating of players and photo of a player's box

The software application for exchanging puzzle pieces was developed solely for the experiment. It consisted of a browser based application, by which participants could arrange and exchange pieces via drag and drop. Figure 15 shows a player's scree with the software application, consisting of different inboxes for received pieces and one solution box in the upper left corner, to arrange a solution square. Communication between players was conducted via the group chat function of the software Skype[©]. Accounts were created with the names Player1-Player5.

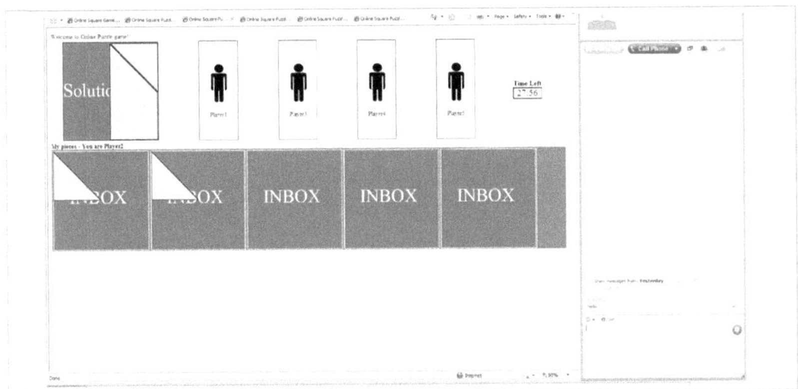

Figure 15: Screen as the player sees is during the game

The left part shows the browser application for exchanging puzzle pieces. The right part of the screen the group chat functionality via Skype.

Side note – a detailed description of experimental software

It has been mentioned that OCI communities interact in a virtual setting. Therefore the experiment should resemble this environment as closely as possible. One challenge for the experiment was to transfer Bavela's puzzle game, which was originally played in a real-life environment with puzzle pieces out of paper, to a virtual one.

The technical realization involved a high degree of specific programming skills. Therefore I chose to outsource the programming of the specific software. However, I designed the specific requirements for the software application and conducted the testing. After designing the software I posted the detailed requirements on a platform for freelance programmers, namely *freelancer.com*. After reviewing different offers I chose a programmer based on the recommended price and prior experience of the programmer. Details were discussed and clarified via several Skype calls. The development phase lasted about eight days, which was followed by a testing and reworking phase, in which different bugs were identified and corrected.

The software consists of two components, a central server unit (PHP 5.2 / MySQL) and different clients running on JavaScript and HTML (see Figure 16).

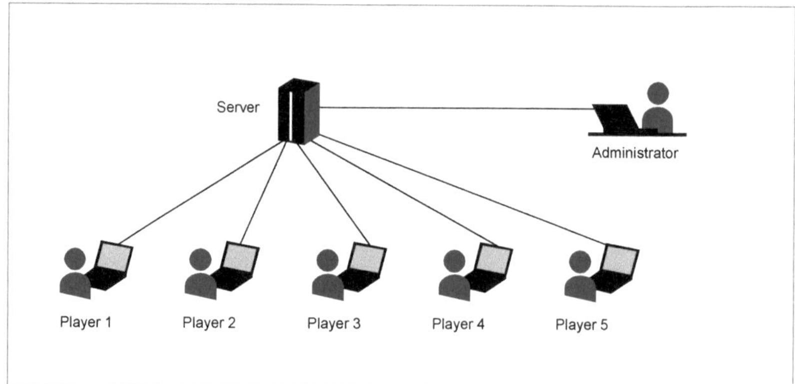

Figure 16: One server and the six clients of software application

Each client consists of a log-in page with a drop-down menu to choose options ranging from *player* number *1-5* to *administrator*. The administrator screen consists of three features. Five icons of player 1-5, indicating which player is logged in, a *start, stop* and *reset* button and a field where the game time could be entered. The page for players also consists of three main elements (see Figure 17). (1) Five *inboxes* where puzzle pieces that are traded appear. The number of inboxes is limited to five, because the software was programmed in a way, to restrict the number of pieces a player could possess to five. The choice for this restriction is made, to sustain the collaborative aspect of the game. Otherwise it would be possible to send all pieces to one player who would then solve the puzzle locally and pass out the solution block-wise. Within the inboxes pieces can be rotated in a 90° angle by double clicking on them.

The second (2) component consists of four icons of other players. By pulling a piece via drag-and-drop onto a player icon, pieces are exchanged. Once a piece is pulled onto the player icon and the mouse released, the piece disappears from the player's screen and appears in one of the inboxes of the corresponding player.

The upper left corner of the screen shows a (3) solution box. Pieces can be freely arranged in the solution box to form a square. However, pieces within the solution box are still in the possession of a player, this means, that a player cannot receive more than five pieces by storing some in the solution box. The screen is completed by a counter showing the remaining (4) game time. Figure 17 shows a screenshot with the different components.

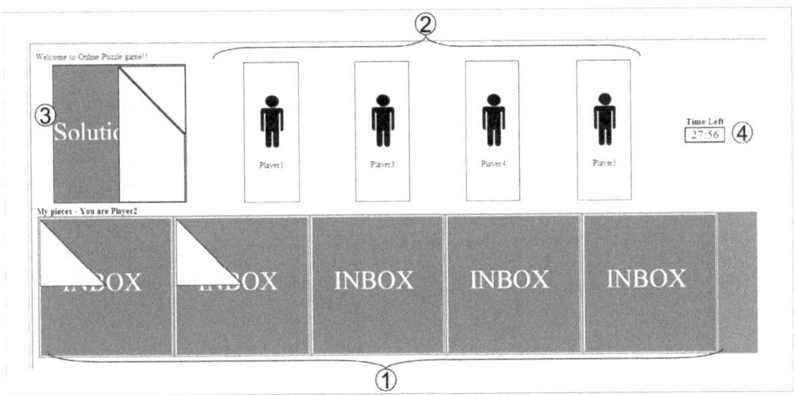

Figure 17: Detailed overview of components on a player's screen

After logging on a player sees the screen as described, but no pieces are apparent. Only after the administrator starts the game, pieces appear in the inboxes. The allocation of pieces was always the same according to Bavela's original setup (see Figure 12).

Piece	Sender	Recipient	Time sent
A-3	Player2	Player1	11:12:02
H	Player1	Player2	11:12:03
G	Player1	Player2	11:12:04
A-2	Player2	Player1	11:12:27
C-1	Player2	Player1	11:12:29
F-2	Player5	Player4	11:12:48
A-3	Player1	Player2	11:13:46
A-2	Player1	Player2	11:13:47
C-2	Player5	Player1	11:14:07
C-2	Player1	Player3	11:14:10
C-1	Player1	Player3	11:14:12
F-2	Player4	Player3	11:14:52
B	Player5	Player1	11:15:39

Table 7: Example of standardized log file post to the game (excerpt)

The interaction behavior of players is measured via the $Pieces_{sent}$ (see Chapter 4.3.4). To record this variable a standardized log file is written after every game. However, some pieces are identical in shape and size (e.g. four rectangular triangles). To allow a distinctive tracking each piece is named with a unique identifier, for example labeling the four rectangular triangles A-1, A-2, A3, A-4. Once the game ends or is stopped by the administrator a log file, consisting of pieces exchanged, is written. The file consists of information about the sender, recipient, the piece sent, time sent and the distribution at the end of the game. Table 7 shows a sample of a log file written after a game.

5.1.2.3 Sampling of subjects and groups

Subjects for the experiment were students from an engineering management program from the Hamburg University of Technology. Participation was voluntary, however students were awarded with an improvement of 0.3 on the final exam grade for participating in the experiment.[33] Students were given a list of possible dates and asked to mark any date they would be willing to attend. From the list groups of five were formed, however subjects were randomized to prevent registration of cliques, where participants knew each other in advance. For the same reason email invitations for the experiment were sent via blind copy. For participation in the experimental study 76 for students initially signed up. However, since the experiment requires five participants to be present at the same time only 14 experimental sessions could be scheduled due the lack of availability for proposed dates. Therefore 70 students were invited for participation. The 6 remaining students served as a back-up in case of no show or short notice cancelation of participants.

5.1.2.4 Control variables, data collection and sample

Data was gathered from two sources: individual factors of participants (key factors), such as perceived *Motivation* and *Procedural Justice* were collected via a questionnaire post the experiment.[34] Information concerning interactions (e.g. participation during game) and outcome measures (performance of players) were collected through log files routinely written in a standardized file post the game. The log files consist of

---

[33] 0.3 points on an exam grade reflects a 5% improvement on the final grade.

[34] For the questionnaire and used items see Chapter 4.3.2 and appendix.

information about send pieces, sender player, recipient player and time the piece was sent (see Table 7).

Furthermore chat messages, including information about sender at time sent, were recorded to allow qualitative analysis of player's interaction. Table 8 shows an example of recorded chat messages.

Time	Sender	Message
[10:40:46]	Player1	projekt leiter ? bin für ja
[10:41:20]	Player4	jop
[10:41:23]	Player3	alles klar
[10:41:39]	Player1	dann rnit auswahl oder abstimmen?
[10:41:39]	Player2	ja, mit projekt leiter
[10:41:51]	Player3	ich bin für player 1
[10:41:57]	Player5	Dann sind wir einstimmig
[10:42:06]	Player4	player 1

Table 8: Sample of recorded chat messages (excerpt)

All 14 sessions including 70 participants were conducted. One person did not show, but was replaced by a back-up participant. One of the 14 sessions had to be aborted during the experiment due to technical difficulties with the software. Therefore the sample used for the analysis consist of 65 participants (35 for treatment $A_{endog,}$, 30 for Treatment B_{exog}).

Control variables

Control variables are included to rule out alternative explanations, however a central premise is that they shall be treated as important as independent and dependent variables (Becker, 2005). It must be therefore carefully considered which measures to include as control variables for the study.

Since communication between participants occurs solely via chat different typing speeds may influence group communication. If a players typing speed extremely exceeds his teammates, he may be able to dominate a discussion which again may affect measured variables like *Motivation*. Consequently *Typing Speed* is introduced as a control variable, by measuring the time participants take to typewrite a standardized sentence at the end of the experiment. Another factor that might influence communication is language skill. Although all participants should have similar language skills, since they are chosen from one sample of students, some students are not native German speakers. Because communication during the game is taking place in German, this might have a certain influence. Therefore *Native Language* is introduced as a second control variable.

Even though the inclusion of demographic control variables is criticized if no theoretical relationship is expected (Spector & Brannick, 2011) still the majority of studies include information like gender and age. For the sake of completeness *Gender* and *Age* make up the last two control variables.

5.1.3 Instructions and experimental manipulation

There are two phases for the experiment: First a group discussion and then the actual game when teams try to solve the puzzle. The second phase, the handling of puzzle task has been described in the previous chapter. Manipulation is taking place during the first phase with two different treatments. Before the group starts playing the task they are asked to engage in a group discussion. Depending on the treatment the group discussion involves two aims which are described in the manipulation section of this chapter. First the instructions which are identical except for one paragraph (see below) for both treatments are presented.

Instructions

Upon arriving participants were all given the instructions with following text[35]:

> ***Goal of the game***
> *You are participating in a group puzzle exercise. Goal of the game is to form your own square out of different puzzle pieces. In order to form a square you have to exchange pieces with 4 other players who are participating in this game.*
> *During this game you will be able to earn points, depending whether you and the other players in your group are able to form a square. The 5 players with the most points will receive an Amazon voucher worth 20€. There will be other groups of 5 playing this game. So your points are compared with your 4 group members and all players of the other 15 groups (see `Point allocation` section how points are allocated)*

---

[35] Instructions also included a timeline of the experiment and some basic information how to use the tool. For details see complete instructions in the appendix A.

Procedure of game

Start:
At the beginning of the game every player has a set of pieces in his Inboxes. (The pieces will appear once the game is started, so the boxes are now empty)

Forming squares:
Within the Inboxes pieces can be rotated by double-clicking on them. In the upper left corner every player will find an individual Solution box. To form your own square you must move pieces from one of the Inboxes via drag-and-drop to the solution box. Within the Solution box pieces can be arranged freely (Do not worry too much about perfect alignment of pieces). The Solution box has the same measurements as your square must have.

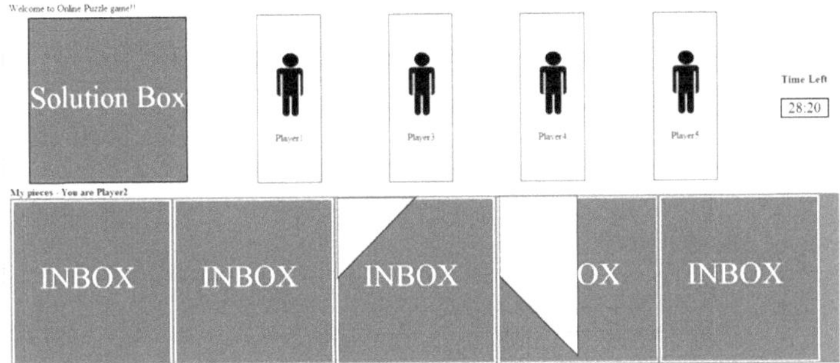

Exchanging Pieces:
In order to give pieces to other players you have to move the piece via drag-and-drop onto the player. Pieces you receive will appear in one of the Inboxes. Notice that you can only hold 5 pieces. If you reach that limit you are not able to receive further pieces.

Possible solutions:
Out of the pieces distributed among the 5 players squares can be formed in many ways. However if five squares must be constructed out of the pieces there is only one arrangement that can succeed (5 squares are possible!). This also means, while you already accomplished a square, you might block other solutions if you do not have the perfect solution and are not willing to exchange pieces anymore.

Communication & time:
Once the game is started you will be able to chat via Skype with the other players. Do not use real names during the chat, address each other only by player number. You will have 40 minutes to solve the task. If you finish early you may signal this to the administrator who will end the game.

Point allocation

The allocation of points you receive depends on your individual and group performance. After 40 minutes there will be a count of how many squares your group was able to form (Counted are the squares in each Solution box – each player can only form one square). Based on the count each player will be given a number of points which are calculated by following formula:

20 points for your square + Number of total group squares (including your square) x 10 Points

Hence you can reach 0 to 70 points, depending on how many squares your group is able to form and whether your individual square is among them. For demonstration payoff table below.

Number of total **group squares** formed

	0	**1**	**2**	**3**	**4**	**5**
Own square	N/A	30	40	50	60	70
No own square	0	10	20	30	40	N/A

Payoff Table

Remember that your points are also compared with other groups. If there are more than 5 participants with the same number of points, the group time needed to reach the solution will be taken into account.

Manipulation

The instructions for treatment $A_{end.}$ (endogenous rules) included following paragraph at the end of the instructions:

*Before the 40 minutes are started by the administrator you have **15 minutes as a group to discuss a set of rules** that might help you to come to better results as a group. The list of rules will be given to you before the discussion starts.*

The list of rules a team could choose from was presented as a print out of two set of rules to choose from (for detailed list see Chapter 4.3.3 or appendix B). The list of rules included further information about the process of how to agree on the rules:

Before you start to play the game you have to choose some rules that might help you perform better. Choose your rules carefully they can effect the outcome of the game significantly. For each block one rule has to be chosen. You have 15 minutes to discuss the rules as a group and come to a consensus. At the end of the 15 minutes the administrator will ask the group via Skype about the choice.

For treatment $B_{exog.}$ the text within the instructions was replaced by following:

> *Before the 40 minutes are started by the administrator you have **15 minutes as a group to discuss any topic you like**. During the 15 minutes the administrator will give you some more directions.*

7 minutes into the group discussion the administrator announced following message via the group chat:

> *In course of the game a set of rules has to be followed. The set of rules will be passed out now.*

The administrator then handed the list of rules (again in paper form), which were chosen by the correspondent team under treatment $A_{end.}$. If the list implied the rule of voting a project leader (1a), the group was asked at the end of the 15 minutes about their choice. The reason for introducing the rules under treatment $B_{exog.}$ after 7 minutes and not at the beginning of the 15 is as follows. The main idea is to avoid that rules are apprehended as part of the game instructions, consequently the temporal separation is believed to assist to this objective. Secondly the alteration of complete freedom within the first 7 minutes, compared to the indoctrination of rules is supposed to make the manipulation stronger. The reason of introducing the rules in the middle of the 15 minutes and not at the end has practical reasons. One is that players obviously take some time to understand the meaning and implications of the rules. Secondly, a certain rule configuration required also groups under treatment $B_{exog.}$ to agree on a project leader which requires time.

To agree on rules a group of five hardly needs the full 15 minutes. After having agreed on the rules the group under treatment $A_{end.}$ therefore also had time to discuss other topics, for example solution strategies how to solve the task. This is important to acknowledge for a balanced design. Otherwise group $B_{exog.}$ could be biased towards building a group identity and thus be more likely to cooperate.

5.1.4 Procedure of Experiment

Upon arriving for the experimental session participants were randomly seated in the different booths in front of a computer terminal. Participants were then advised to read the instructions, which were placed next to each computer terminal. After having read the instructions a short movie explaining the use of the tool and communication via chat was shown. The choice for a movie rather than given verbal instructions is to reduce possible framing effects as much as possible. The time for the group discussion was started by the administrator by announcing it over the group chat. The group discussion was conducted in German. If the group did not announce the choice of rules by itself, the administrator asked for the group choice at the end of the 15 minutes (only treatment $A_{end.}$). For treatment $B_{exog.}$ the administrator announced the initiation of rules to obey after 7 minutes.

For both treatments time checks were announced by the administrator 3 minutes before the 15 minutes ended. Furthermore different standard answers for possible upcoming questions were prepared. For example the question for consequences of non-compliance of rules would have been answered a follows:

> *You have to follow the rules. Any violation of rules will be reviewed after the game and might lead to consequences concerning the rating.*

If the player or group persisted on knowing the precise consequences following answer would be given:

> *We cannot give the precise consequence at that moment since it depends on the review after the game.*

Such events would be marked in the experimental protocol for each session. However, no such inquiries occurred during the experimental sessions.

After the group discussion the game was started by the administrator. With beginning of the game pieces appeared on the screen of the players. After 40 minutes, or when a team accomplished the optimal solution prior to that, participants were asked to fill out a questionnaire. Finally the control variable *Typing Speed* was recorded by letting participants type one standardized sentence.

6 ANALYSIS AND RESULTS

Group behavior is complex with many aspects to consider. To fully understand and investigate as many aspects as possible resorting to one research method may not be sufficient. Generally a distinction between a quantitative and qualitative approach can be made. Especially in the social science the use of multiple methods has been advocated, since the mix of qualitative and quantitative methods is complementary and compensates for the specific weaknesses of each method (cf. Jick, 1979).

Such a mixed approach – combining quantitative and qualitative methods – is chosen in this dissertation project. Yet the focus lies on a quantitative analysis of the experiment, in order to answer the main research question. The use of qualitative methods complements the quantitative analysis to support the quantitative findings and gain a deeper understanding. Analyses are divided in three interconnected but separate studies. Quantitative methods are employed for study 1 and 2. For study 3 qualitative methods are used. Methodology fundamentals and considerations are explained prior to the studies.

6.1 Quantitative analysis – choosing appropriate tests

To test hypotheses appropriate statistical tests have to be chosen. Selecting the right test depends highly on the collected data such as the scales used and its distribution. Furthermore relationships between variables should be derived properly to test causal relationships.[36] The design of the experiment calls for two separate statistical studies. The first study – and the centre of attention of this thesis focuses on the effect the manipulation of exogenous vs. endogenous governance rules has on the key factors, namely motivation, perceived conflict and justice, of participants. The second study centers the outcome measures of the conducted experiment and investigates how the key factors (dependent variables from study 1) are associated with outcomes such as interactions between participants and performance of the group. Consequently the

---

[36] See Chapter 4 for the derived research hypotheses and testing model.

dependent variables from study 1 function as independent variables in study 2. Figure 18 gives an overview over hypothesized relationships of variables for study 1 and 2.

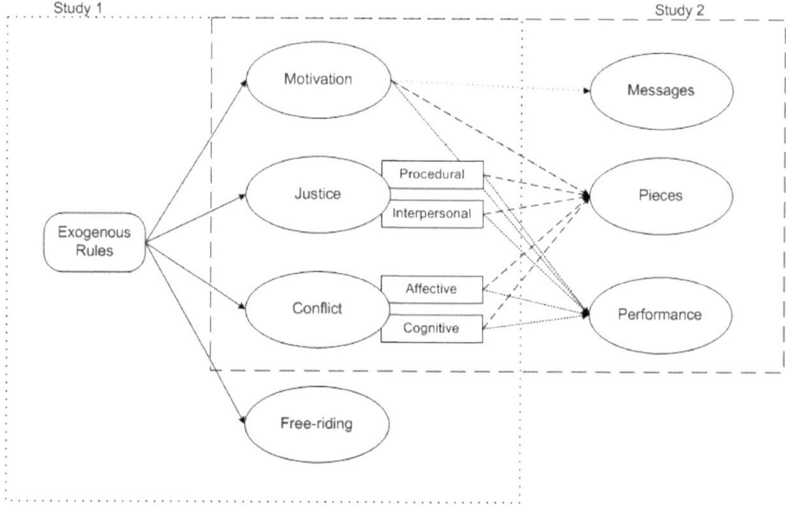

Figure 18: Assumed relationships between variables as stated in the hypotheses
Different types of arrows represent separate statistical analysis.

Choosing the appropriate statistical tests

After examining the given variables for study 1 it is evident that the sole independent variable shows a nominal scale (Treatment A / B) while the six dependent variables – measured via the questionnaire – have a metric scale. With regard to the nature of the existing variables it seems appropriate to choose an analysis of variance, more specific a multivariate analysis of variance (MANOVA):

> "It is a dependence technique that measures the differences for two or more metric dependent variables based on a set of categorical (non metric) variables acting as independent variables." (Hair, 2010: 439)

Analysis of Variance (ANOVA) and its extension (MANOVA) are the standard tests when it comes to experimental designs (Backhaus, 2008; Hair, 2010). As mentioned before the scale used for dependent and independent variables are in line with the requirements for a MANOVA. However, examining the nature of the scale for *Free-riding* more closely it becomes apparent that it differs from 'regular' metric scales in that the arithmetic mean of a group is always 40. Since respondents are always required to allocate all 40 points across the group, no deviations of means between groups are possible. Considering that analysis of variance depends highly on the sum of squared deviations the variable of *Free-riding* is excluded from the MANOVA. *Free-riding* is analyzed using a test of variance, which is in line with authors who applied the same scale prior (see Brooks & Ammons, 2003).[37]

The focus of study 2 is the association between individual factors such as *Motivation* and perceived *Justice* with outcome measures like behavior and performance of the group. Therefore the former five dependent variables from study 1 now function as the independent ones – the dependent variables are the three outcome measures *Messages_sent*, *Pieces_sent* and *Performance*. To analyze the association between these variables, multiple regression is the appropriate statistical technique:

> "Multiple regression analysis is a statistical technique that can be used to analyze the relationship between a single dependent (criterion) variable and several independent (predictor) variables." (Hair, 2010: 161)

Hair adds that regression is best applied "[...] when both the dependent and independent variables are metric." (Hair, 2010: 162), a criterion which the present variables satisfy. Recognizing the prerequisites of multiple regression and the formulated hypotheses three separate multiple regression analysie are run – apiece for the three dependent variables *Messages_sent*, *Pieces_sent* and *Performance*.

6.1.1 Data sample

Responses of 65 participants were included in the sample. Thereof 11 (17 %) were female and 54 (83%) male respondents. Average age was 25, ranging from 22 to 30. Concerning the educational background of respondents the sample was exceptionally homogenous, since all participants were from one course of studies. Most respondents of the sample 57 (88%) declared German as their native language, while 8 (12%) grew up with a different language. However, it can be stated that German language skills of non-native speakers could be considered sufficient since they attended lectures in German.

---

[37] For details about analysis of *Free-riding* see Chapter 6.2.2.

Since my sample consists of students I want to justify why I believe it to be suitable. According to Stevens (2011) a student sample is appropriate if the underlying universalistic theory applies to all population and is not specific to one context. Since my hypotheses are derived from general theories of motivation or justice, I believe them to be applicable to any population. Van Rijnsoever et al. (2012), also resorting to the work of Stevens, state a further justification for a student sample: Using a homogenous sample optimizes the internal validity (van Rijnsoever, Meeus, & Donders, 2012). Another point is that the sample is overwhelmingly male. Since I did not expect any effects of gender this should not reduce the validity of the experiment. Anyhow gender is included as a control variable, to investigate any unwanted effects. I want to conclude with one last point. OCI communities exist in many different forms, assembled of homogenous groups such as communities of doctors or very heterogeneous groups, for example contributors of Wikipedia. Therefore any other data sample would not be inherently better or worse than the chosen student sample.

6.1.2 Data preparation

In order to conduct a MANOVA and multiple regression analyses different assumptions have to be met. Many assumptions apply to both statistical tests and can be therefore investigated at the same time. The data is tested to rule out severe violations of those assumptions that would make the use of MANOVA and multiple regressions unfeasible. Furthermore since variables are measured with different items the chosen constructs are investigated to ensure reliability.

Verifying constructs from questionnaire items

When one uses constructs summated by multi-items, these constructs should be investigated for reliability in order to assure that the items measure the desired construct. First I ensure reliability of the items by analyzing cronbach's alpha and corrected item- total correlation as proposed by Bühl (2006). Corrected item- total correlation is considered to be the most important measure to assess the usefulness of items by calculating the coefficient of correlation between the item and the mean of the scale (Bühl, 2006). Examining the item- total correlation for my data set, no item shows vast anomaly which would justify a removal from the scale (see Table 9).

Since the constructs are measured with different number of items (ranging from 3 to 8) dissimilar degrees of reliability are accepted, because as the number of items increases so does the expected reliability (Lewis-Beck, 1994).

Construct	Item	Scale Mean if Item Deleted	Scale Variance if Item Deleted	Corrected Item-Total Correlation	Cronbach's Alpha if Item Deleted
Motivation Cronbach's Alpha:.787	mot_1	37.89	27.629	.503	.766
	mot_2	38.28	27.610	.330	.788
	mot_3	37.69	25.060	.640	.742
	mot_4	38.29	24.054	.615	.743
	mot_5	37.71	28.241	.290	.793
	mot_6	37.62	26.709	.525	.761
	mot_7	38.42	22.028	.670	.730
	mot_8	38.34	24.196	.449	.777
Affective Conflict Cronbach's Alpha:.896	conf_aff_1	6.03	7.999	.860	.830
	conf_aff_2	5.92	9.228	.790	.860
	conf_aff_3	6.08	8.947	.732	.879
	conf_aff_4	5.51	9.129	.704	.889
Cognitive Conflict Cronbach's Alpha:.857	conf_cog_1	4.28	3.360	.693	.833
	conf_cog_2	4.03	3.187	.709	.819
	conf_cog_3	4.06	2.871	.791	.738
Procedural Justice Cronbach's Alpha:.643	just_proc_1	11.35	5.170	.484	.529
	just_proc_2	11.22	6.109	.375	.607
	just_proc_3	11.18	5.090	.455	.552
	just_proc_4	11.06	6.121	.385	.601
Interpersonal Justice Cronbach's Alpha:.750	just_int_1	12.94	4.184	.566	.681
	just_int_2	12.95	4.576	.689	.637
	just_int_3	12.80	4.413	.571	.679
	just_int_4	13.14	4.309	.423	.777

Table 9: Cronbach's Alpha and Corrected Item-Total Correlation for constructs

Comparing cronbach's alpha for our constructs to the proposed expected reliability table for different number of items by Lewis-Beck all pass the test.[38]

Even when applying the stricter value of 0.7, which is considered to be sufficient by most authors (Kent, 2001) all constructs, except for *Procedural Justice* (0.643) pass the test. However, taking into account the small number of items and the closeness to the threshold value of 0.7 it is fair to testify a reasonable reliability for all constructs.

Since I am using established constructs an exploratory factor analysis is dispensable yet a confirmatory factor analysis (CFA) can be useful. A confirmatory factor analysis in contrast to an exploratory one is chosen if variables are based on theoretical considerations, where a researcher wants to test a hypothesis rather than generate one (Backhaus, 2008). Referring to Bühl (2006), I conduct a factor analysis using principal components extractions and rotating factors via varimax. Within the rotated component matrix values smaller 0.3 are suppressed. Examining the rotated component matrix most items show loadings >0.6. Nevertheless some cross-loadings can be observed (see Table 10). Most cross-loadings are easily explicable since the higher constructs of justice and conflict are measured by subordinate ones. Therefore a correlation between the subordinate one – and therefore correlations between items of secondary constructs (as observed with *Cognitive-/Affective Conflict* and *Procedural-/Interpersonal Justice*) can be expected. Loadings of justice related items on the factor conflict and vice versa can be interpreted by drawing on the close relationship between justice and conflict. Only the negative loading of the motivation related item 8 on cognitive conflict remains inexplicable.

After having conducted the refereed tests and taking into account that constructs are well established I refrained from deleting any items. According to common practice constructs are built by calculating arithmetic means of the related items (cf. Hoegl & Gemuenden, 2001; DiStefano, Zhu, & Mindrila, 2009).

---

[38] Proposed table for *expected reliablity* see Lewis-Beck (1994).

Rotated Component Matrix[a]					
	Component				
	1	2	3	4	5
conf_cog_2	.776	.351			
conf_cog_3	.762	.393			
just_int_3	-.680			.565	
conf_cog_1	.656				
just_proc_3	-.640				.373
mot_8	-.457		.441		
conf_aff_3		.873			
conf_aff_1	.338	.812			
conf_aff_2	.350	.803			
conf_aff_4		.727			
mot_3			.794		
mot_1			.703		
mot_7			.700		
mot_6			.670		.401
mot_4			.603		.307
mot_5		.301	.560		
mot_2			.424		
just_int_1				.826	
just_int_2	-.425			.757	
just_int_4		-.372	.309	.427	.303
just_proc_4				.313	.692
just_proc_2			.336		.619
just_proc_1	-.505				.561

Extraction Method. Principal Component Analysis.
Rotation Method: Varimax with Kaiser Normalization
a. Rotation converged in 9 iterations.

Table 10: Rotated compent matrix for the five main constructs

Sample Size

Hair (2010) defines the required minimum individual group size (per treatment) for a MANOVA greater than 20, however the greater the number of dependent variables the larger the sample has to be. As a practical guide he recommends the sample of each individual group to be larger than the number of dependent variables. Considering the sample size of >30 and the number of 5 dependent variables for the MANOVA the requirement is met. Furthermore the sample is especially homogenous (see Chapter 6.1.1), which is positive for the statistical analysis and requires a lesser sample size. Identifying a sufficient sample size for multiple regression different considerations exist, such as desired power and expected strength of the relationship. Generally a sample size above 50 is sufficient for multiple regression (Hair, 2010), an assumption which is met for my proposed study.

Linearity and Multicollinearity

Before including variables into a MANOVA one ought to test that "[...] the dependent variables should not have high multicollinearity [...], which indicates redundant dependent measures and decreases statistical efficiency." (Hair, 2010: 460).

An indicator for multicollinearity is a high correlation (close to 1) (Backhaus, 2008). The correlation matrix shows no correlations close to 1 between dependent variables. Therefore no problems with multicollinearity are expected (see Table 11).

Inspecting the scatter plot matrix for the five main constructs shows no signs for outliers or curvilinear relationships, infringing the assumption of a linear relationship between the dependent variables (see Figure 19).

Inspection of multicollinearity for the multiple regression is done by investigation of variance inflation factor (VIF), which reveals no issues of such nature (see also Chapter 6.3.2 for more details on the investigated assumption for the multiple regression).

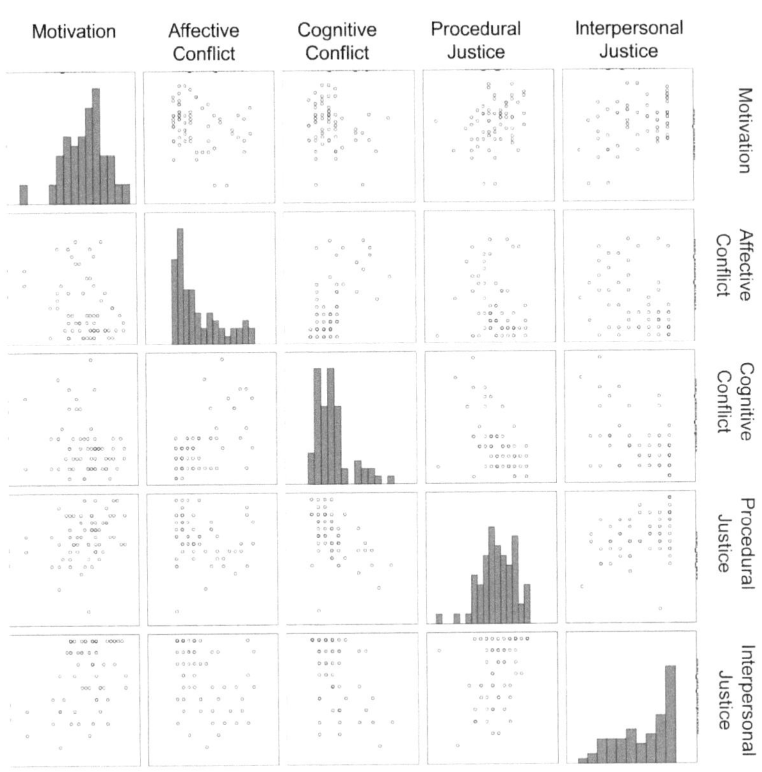

Figure 19: Scatter plot matrix and histograms of the five main constructs used in the MANOVA

Correlations

		Motivation	Affective Conflict	Cognitive Conflict	Procedural Justice	Interpers. Justice	Messages	Pieces	Performance
Motivation	Pearson Correlation	1	-,284*	-,220	,305*	,378**	-,051	-,087	,382**
	Sig. (2-tailed)		,022	,078	,014	,002	,689	,493	,002
Affective Conflict	Pearson Correlation	-,284*	1	,603**	-,204	-,421**	-,023	-,083	-,520**
	Sig. (2-tailed)	,022		,000	,104	,000	,854	,513	,000
Cognitive Conflict	Pearson Correlation	-,220	,603**	1	-,471**	-,473**	-,192	-,021	-,552**
	Sig. (2-tailed)	,078	,000		,000	,000	,126	,868	,000
Procedural Justice	Pearson Correlation	,305*	-,204	-,471**	1	,443**	,169	,098	,287*
	Sig. (2-tailed)	,014	,104	,000		,000	,179	,439	,021
Interpers. Justice	Pearson Correlation	,378**	-,421**	-,473**	,443**	1	-,086	,121	,462**
	Sig. (2-tailed)	,002	,000	,000	,000		,496	,338	,000
Messages	Pearson Correlation	-,051	-,023	-,192	,169	-,086	1	-,037	-,128
	Sig. (2-tailed)	,689	,854	,126	,179	,496		,771	,310
Pieces	Pearson Correlation	-,087	-,083	-,021	,098	,121	-,037	1	,004
	Sig. (2-tailed)	,493	,513	,868	,439	,338	,771		,975
Performance	Pearson Correlation	,382**	-,520**	-,552**	,287*	,462**	-,128	,004	1
	Sig. (2-tailed)	,002	,000	,000	,021	,000	,310	,975	

Table 11: Correlation matrix of variables

* Correlation is significant at the 0.05 level (2-tailed) ;** Correlation is significant at the 0.01 level (2-tailed).
Grey shaded variables are for study 2 only

Normal distribution

One basic requirement for conducting analysis of variance is that variables are normally distributed (Backhaus, 2008). Hence each variable needs to be investigated before analysis of variance can be conducted.

Even though normal-like distribution is a prerequisite for parametric analysis the problem is often neglected since the approach is regularly characterized by a "naive assumption of normality" (Micceri, 1989) where researchers take it for granted. The absence of a consensus for one single measure to test for normality certainly accounts to this ambiguity. When examining whether data follows a normal distribution one has to choose from a wide range of different tests and measures. A straightforward approach to test for normal distribution is to visually investigate histograms of variables. Examining histograms (see Figure 20) indicates departure from a perfect normal distribution for some variables. Consequently further measures shall be taken, to investigate the severeness of the deviation from a normal distribution. The Kolmogorov and Shapiro-Wilk test are suggested in many text books (e.g. Backhaus, 2008). Conversely the Kolomogorov test has faced criticism for its poor power while the better reviewed Shapiro-Wilk test falls short with samples larger than 50 (D'Agostino, Belanger, & D'Agostino Jr., 1990). In order to test for normal distribution I therefore turn to measures of skewness and kurtosis as proposed by different authors (Miles & Shevlin, 2008; D'Agostino et al., 1990).

A perfect normally distributed variable shows a skewness of 0 and a kurtosis of 3 (D'Agostino et al., 1990). When investigating skewness authors differ what deviation can be allowed to still be sufficiently close to a normal distribution. Wright and London (2009) consider a value between -1 and 1 to be satisfactory, while others regard a deviation up to 2 to be acceptable (Miles & Shevlin, 2008).

Miles and Shevlin introduce a further measure, by comparing the standard error of the skew and kurtosis.

> "[...] if the value of a skew or kurtosis (ignoring any minus sign) is greater than twice the standard error, then the distribution significantly differs from a normal distribution" (Miles & Shevlin, 2008: 74).

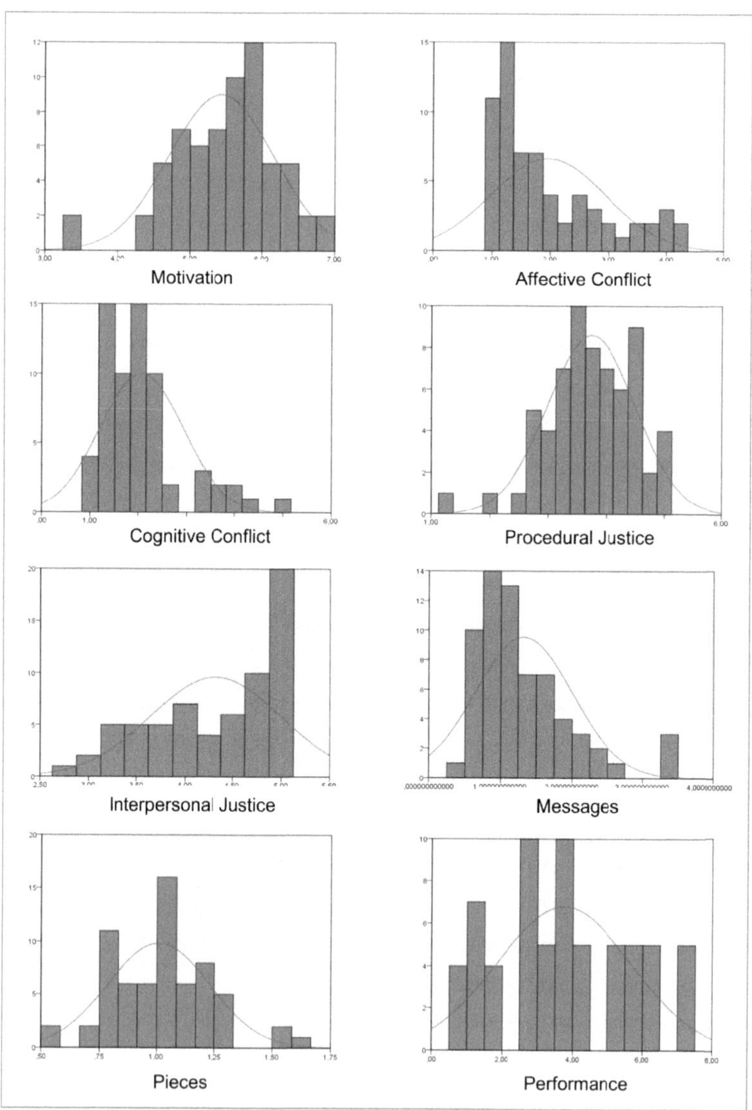

Figure 20: Histograms of variables included in the MANOVA and multiple regression

Variable	Mean	SE Mean	Variance	Skew	SE Skew	Kurtosis	SE Kurt.
Motivation	5.433	0.088	0.509	-0.586	0.297	0.690	0.586
Affective Conflict	1.962	0.121	0.948	1.026	0.297	-0.118	0.586
Cognitive Conflict	2.062	0.106	0.732	1.429	0.297	1.988	0.586
Procedural Justice	3.735	0.093	0.558	-0.562	0.297	0.801	0.586
Interpersonal Justice	4.319	0.083	0.448	-0.608	0.297	-0.912	0.586
Messages	1.321	0.084	0.456	1.488	0.297	2.315	0.586
Pieces	1.008	0.027	0.047	0.281	0.297	0.568	0.586
Performance	3.751	0.235	3.594	0.140	0.297	-1.033	0.586

Table 12: Values for mean, skewness, kurtosis and associated standard errors for used constructs

Examining the variables on the basis of the proposed quality criteria for skewness five out of the nine variables (*Free-riding* is excluded from the MANOVA) are close to a normal distribution with values below 1/-1. Three variables have greater values than 1. However, *Affective Conflict* (1.03) is close to the threshold of 1. Taking the standard error of skew and kurtosis – as proposed by Miles – into account it can be stated that five variables fail the test. However, comparing the variables against the more tolerant threshold of 2, all pass the test and a sufficient normal distribution can be confirmed.

The assumption for multivariate analysis of variance (MANOVA) is not only a normal distribution of the overall sample but a multivariate normal distribution. I therefore tested both treatments groups separately for normal distribution applying the same measures for skew and kurtosis. For treatment $A_{end.}$ (endogenous rules / N=35) all variables show a skew <1. The second group for treatment $B_{exog.}$ (exogenous rules / N=30) show inferior values: Two variables are <1, one (*Affective Conflict* = 1.69) is clear above 1 but still in line with the more tolerant threshold of 2. Only for the variable *Cognitive Conflict* (2.54) a severe violation of the normal distribution can be noticed. I will discuss how I deal with this issue in the next but one paragraph.

Homogeneity of variances

Another assumption for analysis of variance as well as for multiple regression is homogeneity of variances (homoscedasticity). Investigating scatterplots of the individual variables show no signs for heteroscedasticity for the depend variables included in the multiple regression.

Variables included in the MANOVA show no clear picture at first sight. Therefore I tested for homoscedasticity using Levene's test for variance (Howell, 2010). The test reveals significance for three variables (*Motivation, Affective Conflict, Interpersonal Justice*) meaning that homogeneity of variance is not existent for these variables.

Levene's Test of Equality of Error Variances				
	F	df1	df2	Sig.
Motivation	4.227	1	63	.044
Affective Conflict	7.847	1	63	.007
Cognitive Conflict	2.268	1	63	.137
Procedural Justice	.124	1	63	.726
Interpersonal Justice	5.989	1	63	.017

Table 13: Levene´s test of equality of error variance for variables

Dealing with violation of assumptions

Violation of the homogeneity of variance and multivariate normality assumptions does not eliminate the application of analysis of variance and multiple regression per se. Regarding the violation of assumptions for the proposed multiple regression it can be stated that such analysis proofs to be quiet robust against violation (Backhaus, 2008). The same applies for the proposed MANOVA. Many authors show that analysis of variance is robust to violations on the assumption of normality and homogeneity of variance, however a sufficient and close to equal sample size has to be chosen (Bortz & Weber, 2005; Howell, 2010; Hair, 2010). Since my sample consists of a two nearly equal groups with a sufficient size I therefore, after testing for multivariate normality and homogeneity of variances feel confident to advance with further statistical test, even though some variables do not show flawless normal distribution and perfect homogeneity of variances. Table 14 gives an overview over tested assumptions and possible mitigations for violation of assumption for MANOVA and multiple regression.

	Assumption	Testing method	Result	Mitigation*
MANOVA	Outliers	Examine data and box plots	No outliers identified	
	Multivariate normal distribution	Tested via measures of skew	No perfect normal distribution for all variables, however within tolerance	Close to equal group size, sufficient sample size (>20)
	Linearity and multicollinearity	Investigation of scatterplots and correlations	No correlations close to 1	
	Homogeneity of variance	*Levene*-Test	Violation for 3 variables	Close to equal group size, sufficient sample size (>20)
Multiple regression	Outliers	Examine data and box plots	No outliers identified	
	Linearity and multicollinearity	Investigation of scatterplots and correlations	No correlations close to 1, linearity between dependent and independent variables	
	Homogeneity of variance	Investigation of scatterplots	No signs of heteroscedasticity	
	Normal distribution	Tested via measures of skew	No perfect normal distribution for all variables, however within tolerance	

* If assumption is violated

Table 14: Overview assumptions for MANOVA and multiple regression and possible mitigations if assumptions were violated

6.2 Study 1: How governance affects motivation, justice and conflict

The main goal of this study is to identify the effects of the manipulation on known key factors for a functioning community. The reason for choosing the factors and measurement has been presented in the prior chapter. All variables are self-reported by the participants and measured via a questionnaire after the experiment.

After having examined the data carefully – as described in the previous chapter – I aim to test the formulated hypotheses from Chapter 4.3.2 applying the proposed MANOVA (see also Table 15 for an overview of hypotheses). As stated before accounting for the particular scale the variable *Free-riding* is excluded from the MANOVA and tested separately (see Chapter 6.2.2).

To enhance the stability of findings, different MANOVAS including control variables and the test of sub samples were conducted. I am also well aware that not all assumptions for MANOVA are perfectly met (see Chapter 6.1.2), although I am still confident to conduct the proposed analysis for the expressed reasons.

#	Hypothesis
H1	*Choosing your own governance rules has a positive effect on Motivation.*
H2	*Choosing your own governance rules has a positive effect on the perception of Procedural Justice.*
H3	*Choosing your own governance rules has an effect on the perception of Interpersonal Justice.*
H4	*Choosing your own governance rules has an effect on Affective Conflict.*
H5	*Choosing your own governance rules has an effect on Cognitive Conflict.*
H6	*Choosing your own governance rules has a positive effect on Free-riding (less Free-riding).*

Table 15: Overview of research hypotheses for study 1

6.2.1 MANOVA – examining the effects on motivation, conflict and justice

An inspection of variables for both treatment groups revealed differences in mean scores. The group under treatment $A_{end.}$ had lower means concerning the constructs of *Motivation* and *Interpersonal Justice*, while the scores for both measures of *Conflict* showed higher means. Comparison of mean scores for *Procedural Justice* showed only minor differences (Table 16 provides a summary of group profiles for each treatment).

	Condition	Mean	Std. Deviation
Means and Standard Deviations			
Motivation	Endogenous	5.23	0.78
	Exogenous	5.68	0.54
Affective Conflict	Endogenous	2.20	1.07
	Exogenous	1.68	0.77
Cognitive Conflict	Endogenous	2.21	0.90
	Exogenous	1.89	0.78
Procedural Justice	Endogenous	3.76	0.71
	Exogenous	3.71	0.80
Interpersonal Justice	Endogenous	4.14	0.72
	Exogenous	4.53	0.54

Endogenous N=35; Exogenous N=30

Table 16: Means and standard deviation of dependent variables detailed for both treatments

In order to test whether these differences proved to be significantly a multivariate analysis of variance (MANOVA) was run for the whole sample (N=65). The MANOVA revealed a significant multivariate main effect for the treatment, Wilks' λ = .798, $F_{(5;\ 59)}$ = 2.986; p = .018, partial eta squared = .202. The power to detect the effect was .826.[39] After having established significance of the overall test univariate effects were examined. Significant univariate effects were obtained for three of the five variables: *Motivation* ($F_{(1;\ 63)}$= 7.035; p < 0.05), *Affective Conflict* ($F_{(1;\ 63)}$= 4.822; p < 0.05) and *Interpersonal Justice* ($F_{(1;\ 63)}$= 5.645; p < 0.05) (see Table 17). The effect sizes, given partial eta squared were strongest for *Motivation*, followed by *Interpersonal Justice* and *Affective Conflict*.

---

[39] The observed power with .826 can be considered sufficient (see Hair, 2010).

Tests of Between-Subjects Effects			
	Mean Square	F[a]	p	η_p^2
Motivation	3.271	7.035	.010	.100
Affective Conflict	4.312	4.822	.032	.071
Cognitive Conflict	1.661	2.315	.133	.035
Procedural Justice	.038	.068	.795	.001
Interpersonal Justice	2.359	5.645	.021	.082

a. df=1,63

Table 17: Univariate tests (between-subjects effects)

Hypotheses H3 and H4 were supported by the outcome of the MANOVA. The directions of the effects indicate that exogenous rules positively influence the perception of *Interpersonal Justice* and the emergence of *Affective Conflict* (less conflict). The direction of the effect for *Motivation* is contrary to the proposed hypothesis H1, indicating exogenous rules to positively affect *Motivation*. This surprising effect was investigated in a further analysis.

Analysis of mediation effect and correlation

The finding for *Motivation* appears to be conflictive to the stated hypothesis. Letting a group choose its own governance rules has a rather negative than positive effect on *Motivation* as indicated by the univariate effect ($F_{(1; 63)}= 7.035$; $p < 0.05$). While at first sight the result looks atypical considering existing research discussed earlier, checking back to the theory on the association of the investigated variables, it becomes evident that a relationship between *Conflict* and *Motivation* may exist that could explain the observed effect. It is known that motivation may be influenced by different contextual factors such as organizational culture (Mitchel & Daniels, 2003). Furthermore, studies show that the relationship between organizational climate and conflict has a major impact on job satisfaction (Walker, Churchill, JR, & Ford, 1977) and negatively impacts performance (de Dreu & Weingart, 2003). Since motivation is an antecedent of performance (Mitchel & Daniels, 2003) and the constructs of job satisfaction and motivation show an overlap (Tietjen & Myers, 1998) it is expected that the association between motivation and conflict may be analogous.

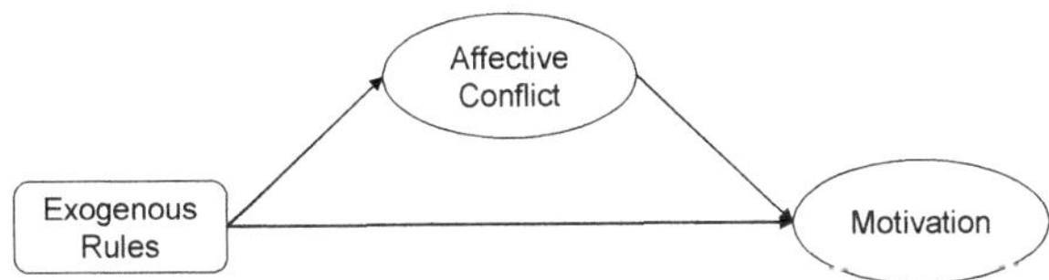

Figure 21: Assumed relationship between manipulation, conflict and motivation

Furthermore analysis of chat interactions of participants during the game supported the theoretical implications (see content analysis study 3). Bearing these findings in mind, a further hypothesis is formulated, investigating whether *Affective Conflict* mediates the impact of the independent variable on *Motivation*.

HYPOTHESIS 18 (H18): *Perceptions of Affective Conflict mediate the effect of exogenous governance rules on Motivation.*

To test this hypothesis an approach by Sapienza and Korsgaard (1996) is applied. Drawing on the work of Baron and Kenny (1986) they consider three conditions that have to be met to support the mediation hypothesis. First, the independent variable must be related to the mediator. This requirement is supported by the previously reported MANOVA, showing a significant effect of treatment on *Affective Conflict*. Second, the mediator must be related to the dependent variables. Examining the reported correlations all relationships between the mediator *Affective Conflict* and *Motivation* are significant (see Table 19). Third, the once significant relationship between independent and dependent variables must be either eliminated or considerably reduced if the mediator is accounted for. This condition is tested by conducting a multivariate analysis of covariance (MANCOVA) introducing *Affective Conflict* as the covariate. Results show that the main effect is no longer significant (p = .058). These findings indicate that *Affective Conflict* may mediate the impact of the manipulated variable (exogenous vs. endogenous) on *Motivation*, supporting the formulated hypothesis H18.

Relationships between dependent variables were investigated by correlations (see Table 19). High correlations between both measures for *Conflict* (p < .01) could be obtained. Measures for justice showed medium correlations (p < .05). *Motivation* correlates highly with *Interpersonal Justice* (p < .01) and on a medium level with

Affective conflict (p < .05) and *Procedural Justice* (p < .05). A further high correlation is the one between *Affective conflict* and *Interpersonal Justice* (p < .01).

Control variables and sub samples analysis

To ascertain that the observed differences were not driven by individuals' differences in *Typing Speed*, *Native Language* and *Gender*, covariate analysis (MANCOVA) was conducted. The results for the MANCOVA revealed no differences in the effects, thus we can be certain that observed differences were not explained by any covariates.[40]

Treatment	Team #	Perfect Solution	Time*
Endogenous	1	Yes	00:18:36
Endogenous	2	No	00:40:00
Exogenous	3	Yes	00:18:22
Exogenous	4	Yes	00:25:17
Endogenous	5	Yes	00:10:00
Exogenous	6	No	00:40:00
Endogenous	7	Yes	00:17:03
Exogenous	8	Yes	00:12:00
Endogenous	9	Yes	00:25:01
Endogenous	10	No	00:40:00
Exogenous	11	Yes	00:20:57
Exogenous	12	Yes	00:12:59
Endogenous	13	Yes	00:11:04

* Net game time (without discussion) in minutes

Table 18: Performance of all teams during experimental sessions

Interestingly the chosen configurations of governance rules under treatment $A_{end.}$ were akin.[41] For example all teams choose to have a project leader and nearly all equipped him with extensive decision power. This fact is important to keep in mind when interpreting the statistical analysis, since no major effects of complete opposite governance configurations (no leader vs. leader) can be expected.

---

[40] A detailed overview over of MANCOVA results is presented in the appendix.

[41] See study 3 (Chapter 6.5.2) for a detailed overview of chosen rules.

Out of the 13 teams 10 were able to reach a perfect solution, 5 under each treatment. Among those teams the average time to reach the solution was 17:08 minutes, ranging from 10 to 25 minutes (see Table 18). Hence differences in performance between teams exist. It is recognized that feedback may have an effect on motivation (Crino & White, 1982; Deci & Ryan, 1996). A form of feedback within the experimental setup is the number of points players obtain for their squares. Being aware of the payoff table of how many points they receive, players can easily asses how well they performed, which consequently may influence their self-reported *Motivation*. In order to evaluate the association of feedback with the dependent variables a sub-sample for further analysis is selected. The sub-sample included all teams which reached a perfect solution since they all received the same feedback through the number of points allocated and the assurance that they reached the perfect solution. The sample consisted of a total of N=50, 25 from each treatment. Again a MANOVA for the sub-sample, analogue to the one run for the whole sample was conducted. The MANOVA for the sub-sample revealed no significant multivariate main effect for the standard significance level of .05. However, an effect for a higher significance level was revealed (Wilks' λ =.794; $F_{(5; 44)}$ = 2.284; p = .063; partial eta squared = .206; observed power = .682). Comparing means and univariate effect sizes given η_p^2 it can be stated that the results for the sub-sample point in the same direction as for the MANOVA of the whole sample. Considering the reduced power for the sub-sample suggests that in order to establish a significance p < .05 would call for a larger sample size. I therefore feel confident that the reported effects are due the manipulation and at most marginal effects of feedback on intrinsic *Motivation* are expected.

Correlation coefficients for relations between dependent variables

Variable	1	2	3	4	5
1. Motivation		-.284*	-.220	.305*	.378**
2. Affective Conflict			.603**	-.204	-.421**
3. Cognitive Conflict				-.471**	-.473**
4. Procedural Justice					.443**
5. Interpersonal Justice					

*p < .05 ; ** p < .01

Table 19: Correlations of dependent variables

6.2.2 Analysis of effects on free-riding

The nature of scale for *Free-riding* makes comparison of mean values between groups useless. For the reason that all 40 points had to be distributed, no difference in means between teams is possible, which makes the application of a MANOVA ineffective. Considering the scale I defined the absence of *Free-riding* within a team (team refers to the five players participating in one experimental session) if all players have a value of 40 points.[42] Consequently a player with less than 40 points can be considered a free-rider, while a player with more than 40 points contributes more than a fair share to the project.

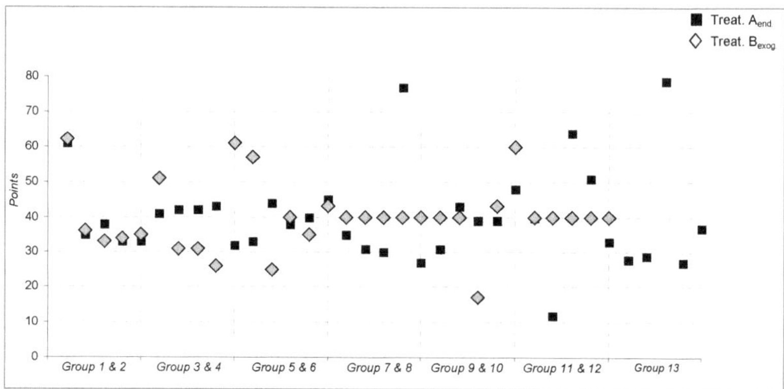

Figure 22: Scatter plot of distributed points per player for *Free-riding*

After examination of the scatter plot diagram (see Figure 22) it appeared that a difference between the two treatment groups exists. Treatment group $B_{exog.}$ showed more players with a score of 40 or higher, meaning no *Free-riding*. A simple measure of frequencies establishs this impression (see Table 20): Under treatment $A_{end.}$ 2 players (5.7%) had exactly 40 points, 13 players (37.1%) showed scores above 40 and 20 players (57.1%) below 40. For treatment $B_{exog.}$ 13 players (43.3%) had 40, 7 players (23.3%) above 40 and 10 (33.3%) below 40. Applying the definition for *Free-*

---

[42] This definition of free-riding is also in line with Tenenberg (2008) and Brooks & Ammons (2003), who used the same scale.

riding one could conclude that the group which could chose their own rules had more free-riders (57.1%) compared to group B (33.3%).

	Median	Variance	% < 40	% = 40	% > 40
Treatment A$_{end.}$ (N=35)	38	180.5	57.14%	5.71%	37.14%
Treatment B$_{exog.}$ (n=30)	40	104.0	33.33%	43.33%	23.33%

Table 20: Key measures of *Free-riding* between two treatments

In order to validate this finding via statistical means I turned to measures of variance. No *Free-riding* within a team (5 players each having 40 points) would mean no variance. Since I was interested whether the reported difference between the two treatment groups proves to be significant, I performed Levene's Test of equality of error variances.

Levene's Test of Equality of Error Variances				
	F	df1	df2	Sig.
Free-riding	1.465	1	63	.231

Table 21: Levene´s test of equality of error variance for variable *Free-riding*

The test indicated that the 76.5 point disparity of variance between treatment group A$_{end.}$ and B$_{exog.}$ was not significantly different ($F_{(1; 63)}$ = 1.464; p > 0.05). Hence, even though a difference of variance between the two groups exists, no support for hypothesis 6 could be established due the lack of statistical evidence.

6.2.3 Discussion

This study examined the relationship between the alternative to choose your own governance rules vs. the indoctrination of external rules on variables like *Motivation, Justice, Free-riding* and *Conflict* within the team. Foremost the findings of this study reveal that indeed a relationship between the two modes of governance (endogenous vs. exogenous) and some of the identified key factors exists.

Interestingly the rules itself were perceived by both groups similar as shown by the means for *Procedural Justice*. This is especially notably since the manipulation between both treatments aimed directly on influencing *Procedural Justice.* Taking a pessimistic view one could argue that the manipulation was unsuccessful, since the manipulation-check for *Procedural Justice* failed to show any effect. Another explanation (which was also supported by the statistical analysis and content analysis of group interaction) is that the rules itself were perceived by both groups as fair, because they helped perform the group better. In that case it may be irrelevant if the rules are given exogenously or endogenously. A similar effect is known from motivation crowding theory, when "[e]xternal interventions *crowd in* intrinsic motivation if the individuals concerned perceive it as *supportive.*"(Frey & Jegen, 2001: 595). Whether the effect of more contradictory rules in the same setting would lead to dissimilar results is a question worthwhile revising in the future.

While the reported effects between the two treatments cannot be clarified by the rules itself, as the absence of differences for *Procedural Justice* indicate, another explanation seems very likely. As described the manipulation itself did not aim at the rules but rather on the process of how they were implemented. However, the process of agreeing on a set of rules can be quiet strenuous. Therefore the source for the reported differences between both treatments lies within this 'electoral process'. As analysis of chat protocols show (see study 3) participants who had to choose rules argued intensely about the different alternatives. Such debates may result in higher levels of conflict and interpersonal friction as indicated by the reported results. This argument is also consistent with the findings of Green and Taber (1980), who affirm that a group decision process leads to high level of interpersonal stress.

The theoretical explanation by Green is also reflected in the data as findings for the other variables indicate. The first finding suggests that teams with the ability to choose their own rules experienced higher levels of conflict – especially for *Affective,* inter-personal related conflicts. Further support is provided by the result for *Interpersonal Justice* which points in the same direction providing further indication that the process to agree on rules leads to interpersonal friction. While the measure for *Free-riding* was not included in the MANOVA frequencies of point allocation and analysis of variance across groups indicate a consistency with the findings for measures of *Affective Conflict* and *Interpersonal Justice.* Members of teams who were able to choose their own rules showed higher variance if rating their team mates, indicating a higher level of discord within the team.

An additional finding presented in the results, is the negative relationship between the ability to choose rules and motivation. A potential explanation is provided through the analysis of the mediation effect of *Affective Conflict* and *Motivation*, which indicates that high levels of *Affective Conflict* may negatively impact the *Motivation*.

The association between *Conflict, Interpersonal Justice* and *Motivation* is also reflected in the correlations between the variables. Correlations indicate that both measures of conflict, namely *Affective* and *Cognitive* have similar effects, indicating that an assumed differentiation between positive and negative conflict is not existent. This finding is in accordance with of the work of Dreu and Weingart (2003). Furthermore *Affective Conflict* negatively correlates with the perception of *Interpersonal Justice*, while *Interpersonal Justice* is positively related to *Motivation*. These results indicate the important association of conflict with success factors such as justice and motivation.

6.3 Study 2: How key factors affect the performance

The first empirical study showed that the choice between exogenous and endogenous governance rules affects conflict, motivation und interpersonal justice. As mentioned before the relationship between factors like motivation and behavior of individuals resulting in performance is of great interest within the research community. The second study therefore aims at answering the second research question by revealing the association of identified key factors of OCI communities, namely motivation, conflict and justice and the behavior of participants and performance. In study 1 I investigated hypotheses 1-6. The following study investigates the remaining hypotheses 7-17.

#	Hypothesis
H7	*Participants Motivation is positively related to the number of Messages$_{sent.}$*
H8	*Participants Motivation is positively related to number of Pieces$_{sent.}$*
H9	*Affective Conflict is negatively related to the number of Pieces$_{sent.}$*
H10	*Cognitive Conflict is negatively related to number of Pieces$_{sent.}$*
H11	*Procedural Justice is positive related to the number of Pieces$_{sent.}$*
H12	*Interpersonal Justice is positive related to the number of Pieces$_{sent.}$*
H13	*Motivation is positively related to the Performance of participants.*
H14	*Affective Conflict is negatively related to the Performance of participants.*
H15	*Cognitive Conflict is negatively related to the Performance of participants.*
H16	*Procedural Justice is positively related to the Performance of participants.*
H17	*Interpersonal Justice is positively related to the Performance of participants.*

Table 22: Overview of research hypotheses for study 2

The relationships between the mentioned factors and the three dependent variables, namely *Messages$_{sent}$*, *Pieces$_{sent}$* and *Performance* were tested with three separate multiple regression analyses.

6.3.1 Impact on sent messages and pieces

To explore whether key factors like motivation are related to the number of messages sent I started with a multiple regression analysis with one dependent variable *Messages$_{sent}$*. Since assumptions for the variables have been previously considered in Chapter 6.1.2 only the overall regression model has to be assessed.

Investigating hypothesis H7, *Motivation* is included in the regression model to predict *Messages$_{sent}$*. The results showed no association between the two variables, therefore H7 is not supported.

Based on the research framework all five independent variables, namely *Motivation, Affective Conflict, Cognitive Conflict, Procedural Justice,* and *Interpersonal Justice* were included in another regression model, now trying to predict *Pieces$_{sent}$*. However, no significant relationship between independent variables and *Pieces$_{sent}$* could be detected. Applying a stepwise estimation approach by including different variables − in the sequence of the correlations with the dependent variable also showed no significant results for any of the independent variables.[43] Consequently I refrained from any further investigation concerning the relationship between factors and $Pieces_{sent}$.

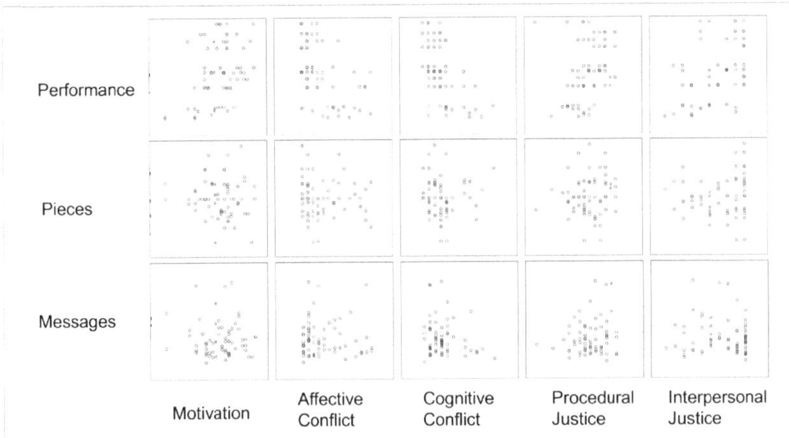

Figure 23: Scatter plots with dependent variables for the three separate regressions represented on the y-axis

It can be concluded that no association between key factors and the variables $Messages_{sent}$ and $Pieces_{sent}$ could be recognized. Taking the weak correlations between independent and the depended variables into account it is reasonable to conclude that indeed no such relationship exists and that lack of statistical proof is not due insufficient sample size or other error. Reasons beyond the statistical conclusion and further explanation are argued in the discussion section of this study.

6.3.2 Impact on performance

Investigating the relationship between key factors and performance I once again included the five independent variables in one regression model with *Performance* as the dependent variable. The analysis indicates that the predictors explain 43% of the variance ($R^2=.428$; $F_{(5;64)} =8.826$; $p<0.001$). *Cognitive Conflict* significantly predicts *Performance* (ß = -.326; $p<0.05$), as does *Motivation* if raising the level of significance (ß = .203; $p<0.1$). Assessing the significant variables using beta weight reveals the highest relative importance for *Cognitive Conflict* followed by *Motivation*.

---

[43] For a detailed overview of stepwise estimation for linear regression see Hair (2010).

Descriptive Statistics and Intercorrelations of Study Variables							
Variable	Mean	SD	1	2	3	4	5
Performance	3.751	1.896	.382**	-.520**	-.552**	.287*	.462**
Independent variables							
1. Motivation	5.432	0.713		-.284*	-.220	.305*	.378**
2. Affective Conflict	1.961	0.974			.603**	-.204	-.421**
3. Cognitive Conflict	2.062	0.856				-.471**	-.473**
4. Procedural Justice	3.735	0.747					.443**
5. Interpersonal Justice	4.319	0.669					

*p < .05 ; ** p < .01

Table 23: Means, standard deviations and correlations for *Performance* and predictor variables

Taken together the results suggest that hypothesis H15 is supported, while results for *Motivation* only weakly support H13. These findings show, that *Cognitive Conflict* negatively predicts the *Performance*, while some evidence exists that *Motivation* positively predicts *Performance*. Support for the remaining hypotheses is not reflected in the data.

The close to equal negative correlations of both types of conflict support the discussed findings of de Dreu and Weingart (2003), that task and relationship conflict are both negatively related to performance (see Table 23).

Coefficients (dependent variable: *Performance*)					
Variable	B	SE B	ß	T	p
Motivation	.539	.291	.203	1.851	.069
Affective Conflict	-.402	.253	-.206	-1.587	.118
Cognitive Conflict	-.722	.311	-.326	-2.324	.024
Procedural Justice	-.109	.306	-.043	-.358	.722
Interpersonal Justice	.464	.349	.164	1.329	.189

Table 24: Regression summary for variables predicting *Performance* (N=65)

Evaluating the variate for assumptions of multiple regression

Although individual variables already have been assessed to meet assumptions of regression analysis in Chapter 6.1.2, it is also of importance to evaluate the variate, in order to validate the estimates. The standard measure for evaluating the regression variate is the residual (Hair, 2010). Assessing the assumption for linearity by analyzing the standardized residual showed no sign of nonlinear pattern (see Figure 24 / right). Certifying that each independent variable's relationship is also linear I investigated the scatter plots (see Figure 19 and Figure 23). No nonlinear pattern could be identified – therefore the assumption of linearity can be confirmed. Investigating again the residual for homoscedasticity in the multivariate showed no pattern of decreasing or increasing residuals, the assumption of homoscedasticity can be verified.

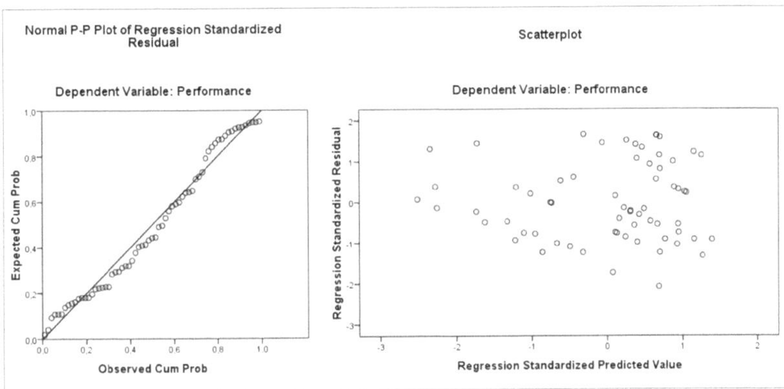

Figure 24: Normal probability plot (left) and scatter plot standardized residual (right)

To test for normality of the error term of the variate I turned to normal probability plots of the residuals. The normal probability plot (Figure 24 / left) showed no values that systematic depart from the diagonal, therefore the residual seems to represent a normal distribution. Furthermore investigation of multicollinearity by inspecting the variance inflation factor (VIF) of variables showed no high correlations that may distort results. Since no assumptions are violated I conclude a sufficient fit of the proposed model.

6.3.3 Discussion

This study has made an effort to establish a relationship between the recognized key factors, namely *Motivation*, *Conflict* and *Justice* within an OCI community and measures of behavior and the actual performance. It has to be stated that no association between those factors and the two measures of behavior ($Messages_{sent}$, $Pieces_{sent}$) could be identified. This missing link is not believed to be due insufficient sample size or measuring fault. Rather I have to acknowledge, that these two measures are not well chosen for a statistical analysis in the given research framework. One reason for this is that the experiment was mainly designed to investigate the effects of the manipulation on the self-reported key factors as done in study 1. The measures for behavior therefore can be somehow seen as a by-product. Besides this weak justification there are explanations while these two measures do not work in the chosen setup. While the quantity of messages sent by a member of a community appears to be an indicator worthwhile investigating in real life communities (e.g. Dahlander & Wallin, 2006), this measure has it limits in an experimental setup. For the variable $Messages_{sent}$ the direction of an effect was complicated to predict. $Messages_{sent}$ could be positively related to motivation, if a player's aspiration to contribute is reflected in a high number of messages. However, the same could be true for a negative relationship, if a player with little motivation voices his frustration through a high frequency of send messages. Considering this argument the limits of pure frequencies of communication are evident. This limitation can be overcome through qualitative methods, going beyond pure frequencies but analyzing the content of sent messages. An attempt is made in study 3.

Another reason is the artificial situation of an experiment. Participants are strained to take part in the game and send messages. Such obligation may exist for many reasons, the presence of a moderator, group pressure of other players, the given time frame to solve the task. A real community is much different to that. Work is done over a long time period, which gives participants the option to resile or get more involved – a behavior which can be detected by the sent messages. Of course an experiment could be designed which accounts for such effects, however this was not the main focus for the designed experiment. The same explanation given for messages may be true for the other variable of behavior $Pieces_{sent}$. Players are subject to the same tension, that is, group pressure or the given time frame. Such tension may be rather a reason why a player sends pieces than a lack of motivation. One conclusion from this study is therefore that simple quantitative measures of interaction behavior between participants have to be treated with care when designing an experiment.

The investigation of key factors with performance proofed to be more fruitful. I have found that *Cognitive Conflict* negatively influences *Performance*. Moreover the significant correlations between both measures of conflict suggest that no difference between beneficial (cognitive) and harmful (affective) conflict exists. These findings follow the explanations laid out by de Dreu and Weingart (2003), who found that both type of conflict negatively impact performance. The results for measures of *Motivation* give some support to the well-established relationship between motivation and performance. The measure for performance in the current study is highly dependent on the overall group performance. Even if an individual is highly motivated, he may still fail to reach an excellent performance if his team members lack a high motivation. Therefore this may explain, while no stronger relationship between motivation and performance could be established. While no significant relationship between measures of justice and performance could be established the correlations between measures of justice, especially for *Interpersonal Justice*, may be an indication for an association of justice and conflict.

6.4 Qualitative analysis

While research questions 1 and 2 have been answered via statistical analysis research questions 3-5 are assessed applying qualitative methods. On the basis of the collected chat messages content analysis is applied. Content analysis is very suitable for analysing "[...] the inference of motivational, mental, or personality characteristics through the analysis of verbal records."(Krippendorff, 2009: 11). This is especially true when it comes to the investigation of interaction processes of groups (cf. Bales, 1976). One important aspect when applying content analysis is the development of a category system to code the different units that are analyzed (Neuendorf, 2010). High-quality categories are the key to a successful content analysis, since "[...] they reflect the formulated thinking, the hypotheses, and the purpose of the study" (Kassarjian, 1977: 12). Categories to answer the proposed research questions can be found within existing literature. The advantage of employing established categories is evident, since they proved to be reliable and are embedded in verified theories. To answer the research questions different category systems are used within this qualitative study. I explain the applied category systems in the subsequent study.

6.5 Study 3: A content analysis of group interactions

Study 1 established a cause-effect relationship between the exogenous governance rules and factors like motivation, conflict and justice while study 2 clarified the association of those factors with performance. Both studies – based on quantitative data gathered during the experiment – were conducted using methods of inferential statistics. For study 3 qualitative methods are employed in order to gain further insights and answer research questions 3-5. Such an approach can help to substantiate the findings from the statistical analysis while at the same time expands possible conclusions.

Each research question is addressed separately using a coding procedure for the chat messages recorded during the experiment.

6.5.1 Response to the manipulation – a content analysis of messages

Results from study 1 are based on the self-reported measures of participants after the game. While this measurement provides convincing data for inferential statistics one disadvantage has to be acknowledged. The self-reported measures after the game only provide a snapshot view, at best an overall perception of the game. Fluctuations of perceptions in course of the experimental sessions are not reflected in the self-reported data. Neither can additional insights nor explanatory approaches for the perception be gained.

Regarding the research question it is not only interesting to evaluate the overall perception but also to pin down the development of variables in certain stages of the game. This is especially true when it comes to the response of a group to the manipulation of imposing exogenously rules vs. letting them decide their own rules. To shed light on this question a content analysis of sent messages during the game promises to be a powerful tool. Since messages sent in course of the game represent a direct and constant stream of participants' emotions and behavior it is possible to identify occurrence of such measure at a certain point of the game, answering the research question 3:

> *How does a community react to exogenously imposed governance rules compared to endogenously chosen rules?*

I first focused on the group discussion, since this is where the manipulation occurred and effects were expected.

Developed codes, data reduction and findings

In order to observe interpersonal behavior of participants an established category system originally developed by Bales (1950) and applied by various authors (cf. Hare, 1973) was used. The category system uses twelve categories to describe the process of interaction of small discussion groups. Six categories constitute social-emotional behavior, *shows solidarity, shows tension release, shows agreement* are positive reactions, while *shows disagreement, shows tension* and *shows antagonism* are negative reactions. These categories are complemented by six further ones related to the task, again divided into two groups: *gives suggestion, gives opinion* and *gives information* as problem solving attempts and *asks for information, asks for opinion* and *asks for suggestion* are subsumed as questions.

Applying the category system to the group discussion, by coding chat messages and interpreting percentage of the code categories in relation to the overall number of messages, teams showed two distinct profiles for both treatments (see Figure 25). Teams who chose their own rules showed distinctly more negative reactions (e.g. disagreement and antagonism), indicating more tension and conflict (on average twice the relative amount for the three categories of negative social-emotional behavior). A further finding is that they showed less solidarity and tension release, like expressions of joy or fun. Comparing task related categories, teams with exogenous rules seemed more goal oriented, engaging more in solution proposal and less in expressing opinion. Applying the content analysis for the course of the game showed group profiles across treatments to be much likewise. These findings support the proposition, that one major source of the measured conflict lies within the group decision process agreeing on a set of governance rules.

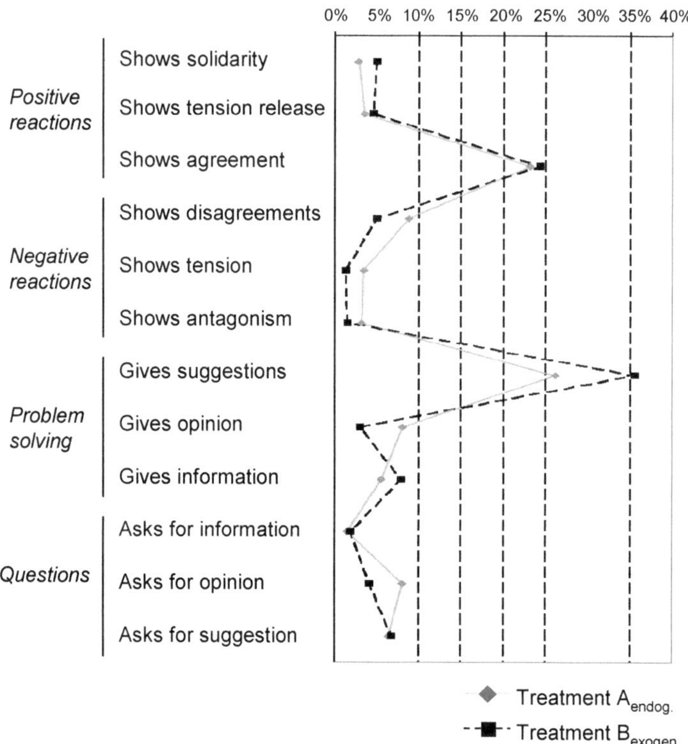

Figure 25: Group profiles of coded chat messages during group discussion

Discussion

Foremost these findings support the proposition that one major source of the measured conflict lies within the group decision process agreeing on a set of governance rules. Comparing the two groups two main differences were apparent. A group who had to agree on rules exchanged more arguments that show negative reactions such as disagreement and antagonism. In an attempt to come to a solution their discussion is characterized by less 'valuable' contributions, such as suggestions, but more voicing of opinion.

Comparing the group profiles for the content analysis led to following conclusion: Most likely participants who chose rules had different preferences (which is also indicated by the content of the messages) for such rules. In the process to combine these preferences into one group decision, those preferences 'clash' and in consequence lead to friction, as indicated by the negative reactions. Since the preference for one rule or another is seldom based on a logical argument, but more that of a personal opinion the problem solving of the group is characterized by more opinion and less suggestions.

A group on the other hand, which is not obligated to agree on rules, can solely focus on the solution of the game. As analysis of content messages show they quickly engage in developing strategies to solve the given task. Their discussion centers around possible solutions and less about personal preferences. This explains the higher amount of problem solving behavior like suggestion and higher amounts of positive reactions. It is likely that the question which strategy or solution approach to take seems less controversial than combining personal preferences for rules. This finding is reasonable considering the relationship between rules and justice, as rules are very much linked to personal perception of fairness (see Chapter 4.3.2.2).

6.5.2 Choice of rules – the desire for leadership

Research question 4 – *Having the choice, does an OCI community prefer a more hierarchical over a grass-root democracy (open) governance style?*– merely applies to teams under treatment $A_{end.}$, since only they had the option to choose from a list of rules. To come to an answer a simple count of chosen governance rules can be conducted. The list of rules a team under treatment $A_{end.}$ could choose from, allowed for 11 different configurations of governance rules. Figure 26 shows the 11 diverse configurations (A-K) that could be chosen. Making an attempt to distinct the configurations into different governance styles following classification can be made.[44] Configurations J and K are considered as a *democratic* style, since all decisions are made by the group. A and E are similar to a *constitutional monarchy* since a project leader exists, but lacks power to make any decisions of importance. B, C, F and G are mixed modes where aspects of leadership and democracy are blended. H can be described similar to a *presidential system* where a leader is once elected and then equipped with vast power. D in contrast resembles more a pure *monarchy*, where a powerful leader is appointed without an election. On the complete opposite side is the

---

[44] The denotation used are aligned with governmental styles used in political science.

last configuration, I, which can be somehow labelled as *anarchy*, since no leadership or decision processes exist. Regarding the two in the research question mentioned extreme poles, it can be generally said that the upper right side of the matrix tends more to a hierarchical governance style whereas the left lower corner is considered as grass-root democracy style.

	Decision rights for exchanging pieces			
	No player can be forced to exchange	Unanimous vote can force exchange	Majority of group can force exchange	Project leader can force exchange
Project leader (determined)	A	B	C (1)	D (1)
Project leader (by group vote)	E (1)	F	G (1)	H (3)
No Project leader	I	J	K	N/A

Figure 26: Different possible rule configurations (letters) and how often they were chosen (numbers)

Evaluating the votes made by the seven teams under treatment $A_{end.}$ it becomes evident that all votes tended to the hierarchical style. All teams chose to have a project leader. Three teams choose configuration H, they choose their own project leader and equipped him with extensive power. Respectively one group each choose configuration D, C, E and G.

Reading these results a first finding is that all teams expressed a desire for leadership since they all chose a project leader. However, the majority of teams (5 of 7) preferred legitimating the project leader by electing him. Only two teams preferred a leader determined by fortune. Another discovery is that most teams (4 of 7) equipped the project leader with extensive decision rights, transferring the power from the group to one leader. Two teams chose to leave the decision rights within the team (majority group vote), while one team preferred no decision rights, either for the leader or the group, therefore leaving decisions to the self-determination of participants. The results indicate (also backed by content analysis of the discussion; see Chapter 6.5.3) that all teams felt that a certain structure, most likely with a strong project leader would progress their performance as a team. This finding is in line with research showing that most open source projects are based on "benevolent dictatorship" (Antikainen, Aaltonen, & Väisänen, 2007). On the opposite the assurance in each others rational behavior or self-organization mechanisms of the team was not very strong. In a nutshell the teams' votes reflect a desire for leadership and the will of participants disengage a great deal of individual decision power.

6.5.3 Development of rules

Even though governance rules play a vital role in the regulation of communities it is known that many implicit rules and norms exist that complement an explicit set of rules (cf. Postmes et al., 2000; Markus, Manville, & Agres, 2000). Hence, I investigated what norms or rules a group creates beyond the explicit governance rules.

The reasons why a team might develop additional rules can be manifold – most likely it might feel that the rules in place are not sufficient or ill fit to serve the task. Since rules and norms are formed within the interaction of the community a content analysis of chat messages was conducted. The focus of this content analysis was the group discussion that took place during the first 15 minutes of the experiment. If additional rules are created it is most likely to happen before the actual game is started and participants are occupied with solving the task. Keeping in mind the experimental setup rules under treatment $B_{exog.}$ are imposed after seven minutes. Therefore it is of interest whether the team develops rules that are similar to the given rules (example project leader) within the first seven minutes.

Development of codes and data reduction

In order to answer the proposed research question, *"What rules or norms are created by the community besides the given set of governance rules?"* a deductive approach for code development was applied. Based on existing research of Ostrom's detailed generic categories for rules exist as well a detailed syntax to describe such rules. A detailed overview of Ostrom's 7 rule categories and syntax has been already described in Chapter 3.3.1.

Rule category	Description	Example from chat protocols
Information rules	Specify the channels used to communicate information among participants, as well as what kinds of information can be transmitted by what positions. There may also be rules specifying required frequency of interaction, or specifying an official language.	"…let´s address each other always with @player xy and so on" (Player4, Group 9, Treat A, Minute 04:12) "A suggestion concerning communication @ all means to address all, otherwise write @PlayerX to address players individually (Player4, Group 5, Treat B, Minute 00:38) "…just one person's talks at a time, you can notice it by hearing him type" (Player3, Group 4, Treat B, Minute 11:41) "…shall we consider a certain way how to describe the pieces (Player5, Group 4, Treat B, Minute 11:44) "…we need clear specifications. For example small triangle as seen on the screen, small square…" (Player4, Group 9, Treat A, Minute 09:24)
Position rules	Define the positions that participants hold. Positions are linked to other rules, equipping the position rule with power.	"i think it's best if p1 does not keep track of the time, because he already has other things to do" (Player5, Group 4, Treat B, Minute 09:21) "all pieces to me, … and I coordinate the pieces" (Player1, Group 5 Treat B, Minute 00:38)
Choice rules	Defines what participants in positions must, must not or may do in their position and in particular point. Choice rules focus on actions. The actions are dependent from the positions and prior actions taken.	"let´s declare, that p1 exchanges with p2" (Player2, Group 4, Treat B, Minute 03:30) "… first each player describes his pieces briefly, then player 1 initiates the exchange of pieces" (Player5, Group 6, Treat B, Minute 10:13) "ok, so all pieces are sent to player 1, …, first 2 pieces, than 3, and so on" (Player3, Group 5, Treat B, Minute 03:08) "…we exchange all pieces in a row, like in a telephone chain…" (Player1, Group 7, Treat A, Minute 02:33)

Table 25: Codes of different rules developed during the game (description column based on Ostrom, 2005, Schweik & Kitsing, 2010)

Therefore the well-established category system was used to identify rules developed by participants. A total of seven different categories exist. However, as the analysis of chat protocols revealed, only three categories could be identified. Therefore only these three categories, including a short description and identified codes matching the categories are presented in Table 25.

Findings

Analysis of chat messages showed that teams under both treatments developed rules to facilitate effective communication. Since communication was conducted via group chat there was an actual risk of confusion when everybody talks at the same time. Information rules regulating communication in a more precise manner could solve this difficulty. Following example shows, that teams created rules to clearly identify the addressee of a message:

> "A suggestion concerning communication @ all means to address all, otherwise write @PlayerX to address players individually" *(Player4, Group 5, Treat B, Minute 00:38)*

A further type of rule developed to make communication more effective was agreeing on an unambiguous language of how to describe specification of the pieces that needed to be exchanged:

> „...we need clear specifications. For example small triangle as seen on the screen, small square..." *(Player4, Group 9, Treat A, Minute 09:24)*

While the information rules described could be found for many teams only two teams developed position rules. An example of a position rule is the project leader – since this rule was part of the explicit set of rules it is evident that no such rule was created by the teams. However one team, before the rules where imposed on them, chose to have a coordinator (with similar tasks than the project leader). Another group tried to create a position rule of a `time keeper´ to unburden the formal project leader from this task:

> „i think its best if p1 does not keep track of the time, because he already has other things to do" *(Player5, Group 4, Treat B, Minute 09:21)*

Another category of rules created by the teams were choice rules. Such rules focus on what action a player must or may take in a certain situation. For that reason they directly relate on how the game is played. Teams argued intensively on how to solve the game, once they agreed on a certain strategy to approach the task choice rules where formulated implying what action a player in a certain position had to take. For example such rules include a certain order in which players had to act:

> "ok, so all pieces are sent to player 1, …, first 2 pieces, than 3, and so on" *(Player3, Group 5, Treat B, Minute 03:08)*

Another case was defining a course of action for each player:

> "… first each player describes his pieces briefly, then player 1 initiates the exchange of pieces" *(Player5, Group 6, Treat B, Minute 10:13)*

Such rules are strongly related to different solution strategies. Since a rule defining an action to be taken is immediately reflected in a certain game strategy (e.g. passing the pieces around clockwise).

Discussion

The analysis of rules developed by participants shows, that groups faced with a complex task feel the necessity to structure and govern interactions with a set of rules. This finding is true whether a group is already provided with rules (under treatment $A_{end.}$) or has no rules at the beginning (as examples for treatment $B_{exog.}$ show). Interestingly all groups developed rules additionally to the explicit game rules that were already in place. This suggests that groups had a strong need for structure and no concern for over-regulation. However, rules developed by different teams all aimed at making communication more efficient and structuring the approach to solve the task. The rules can be considered very goal oriented and involve no high additional costs. For example payoff rules for punishing non-compliance of participants would imply efforts of monitoring that could not be dedicated to the task solution. Conversely, all teams refrained from developing such rules, indicating a trust in each other.

7 DISCUSSION AND CONCLUSION

I started this thesis asking the guiding question whether firms should impose governance rules on a OCI community or rather let it loose by relying on self-governance. I argue that the choice does matter as it has an effect on key factors influencing community interaction and performance. To draw appropriate conclusion and derive recommendations, the findings have to be fully understood, interpreted and the limitations considered.

7.1 Summary of findings

To answer the guiding question I formulated five specific research questions with corresponding hypotheses. Looking at the results, what can be concluded with regard to these questions?

Question 1: Effects of exogenous vs. endogenous rules on key factors

The first and main research question addressed the subject, how exogenous governance rules affect key factors (namely motivation, conflict, justice and free-riding) within an OCI community in comparison to endogenous governance rules. Different hypotheses, stating the assumed relationship between the governance choice and the key factors were formulated and tested via statistical analysis. The results of the quantitative analysis convey several findings.

The ability to choose own governance rules leads to higher levels of conflict. The source of conflict most likely lies within the process of agreeing on rules, when participants engage in controversial discussions which rules to choose. A further indication is that groups who choose their own rules experienced more interpersonal stress, indicated by lower levels of interpersonal justice. While the cause most properly lies in the beginning of the game, namely, the group discussion, the higher level of conflict and interpersonal stress carries throughout the game. There is also some indication that this may lead to less cooperation among participants as indicated by higher levels of free-riding. Another important finding is that the overall motivation is lower if a group chose its own rules. Again, conflict plays a distinctive role, since it influences the motivation of participants negatively. Exogenous rules on the other hand proved to raise less conflict and interpersonal stress, while at the same time where perceived as fair. Less conflict also resulted in a higher overall motivation of participants. In summary, the process of agreeing on rules leads to conflict and interpersonal stress, which in consequences negatively impacts motivation.

Question 2: Association between key factors and performance

The second research question investigated how the key factors, explicitly motivation, conflict and justice are associated with the behavior and performance of participants. For behavior, operationalized by two measures (sent messages and sent puzzle pieces) no relationship is existent. The reason for the absence of any relationship has been stated (see study 2) and is mainly due to the unfortunate measures for an experimental investigation.

For performance a relationship with the key factors exists. Motivation is positively related with the performance. This finding has been proven in numerous contexts and indicates the accuracy of the research model. Furthermore the level of conflict is negatively related to performance, that is, the more conflict, the worse the performance. A relationship that is obvious and consistent with findings from other authors.

While the first research question aimed at establishing a cause-effect relationship between exogenous vs. endogenous governance rules, the second question is a continuation, linking psychological states and attitudes such as motivation and conflict to the behavior and outcome. The difficulty of linking attitudes and the actual behavior is a frequently discussed problem (cf. Stock & Hoyer, 2005).

My results reflect the complexity of linking emotions and psychological states to behavior, however as the findings for performance show, this endeavor has been partly successful. The finding helps to increase the meaningfulness of the overall research model since additional information is provided.

Figure 27 shows an overview of established relationships between variables for study 1 and 2.

Question 3: Reaction of the group to the manipulation

Research question 1 and 2 were answered by analyzing quantitative data after the game, which allowed only for a measurement of the overall perceptions. While many

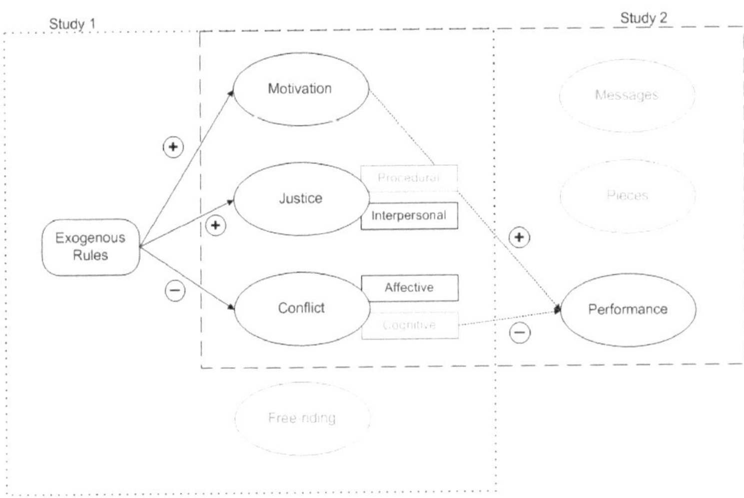

Figure 27: Established relationships between variables after study 1 and 2

conclusions could be drawn from these findings I was interested how the group reacted to the difference of exogenous vs. endogenous rules at the exact point of time. I therefore investigated the group discussion, as the point of time where the manipulation occurred via a content analysis of chat messages. The findings show, that a major source for conflict and interpersonal friction lies within the process of agreeing on rules. Participants who had to choose their own rules showed more negative reactions towards each other and were less focused on a solution, expressing rather opinions than suggestions for solutions. These findings are backed by the fact, that comparison of group discussions during the game (after the discussion) did not show such distinct differences. I therefore conclude that the electoral process of agreeing on a set of rules is likely to influence the interaction behavior and perception of participants significantly. The impact seems so decisive that it affects participants throughout the game, influencing the overall perception and psychological states of participants (see results for question 1).

Question 4: Choice of rules

If a group is faced with the assignment to agree on a set of governance rules, it is of interest what choice they take. Prior work on governance, contrasting more 'open' governance with classical 'closed' modes suggested, that a OCI community would be more likely to prefer an open mode characterized by greater degrees of democratic elements (cf. Markus, 2007). Such a more 'open' mode is characterized by a grass root democracy style rather than classical hierarchies. However, as case study research showed, many communities employ hierarchies, namely having project leader and boards with higher decision rights. Question 4 therefore addressed this issue, asking what choice of rules a group would take when faced with an innovative task. As only groups under treatment $A_{end.}$ were able to choose rules, this question applies only to half of the sample.

Investigating the chosen rules, the finding tends rather towards a more hierarchical style. Groups all chose a project leader and mostly equipped him with extensive decision power. Some groups even discussed further roles, for example the role of a time keeper. As content analysis of the discussion showed, the reason for choosing a project leader was mainly motivated by the expectation of better performance. Participants expressed a desire for leadership in order to help them solve the task better and were willing to transfer individual power to one leader. This finding is consistent with research of OSS communities, which are often based on strong leadership by a benevolent dictator (Antikainen et al., 2007). The results reveal the importance of leadership within OCI communities.

Question 5: Development of rules by the community

An issue which gained interest is the emergence of governance. How and what rules does a group develop to self-govern their actions? Question 5 investigated this matter, by identifying rules beyond the explicit given rules. It is interesting to mention that both groups, no matter if they experienced imposed or self-chosen rules, developed rules of their own. The rules developed by the participants were concerned with structuring information flow more efficient, creating hierarchical positions such as 'coordinator' and defining rules of specific actions for each participant. Such rules directly impacted the solution strategy of each group.

The fact that all groups developed additional rules indicates a strong desire for structure and no concern for overregulation. In sum the additional rules proved to be very goal oriented and were based on mutual trust. For example no monitoring rules to detect and fine non-compliance were developed.

7.2 Limitations and degree of generalization of results

One shall not neglect the limitations of this study. Foremost, as for any laboratory experiment, I faced the restrictions of an artificial setting. This applied to the constructed situation of a game under time pressure, while 'real' life communities exist and evolve over a long time period. Participants in an experiment might be more willing to except appointed leadership for a short period of time than if confronted with it on an everyday basis. Another issue regarding the time aspect is recognizing the extended period it takes for informal relations and norms to develop. Norms like trust and reciprocity play an important role within OCI communities (cf. Lerner & Tirole, 2002; Sulin, 2001). However, within this study I only focused on explicit rules.

Second the chosen sample of students was very homogenous, since they were all from the same age group and professional background. Having such homogenous sample is positive for the statistical analysis of an experimental study because parallelising of groups controls for other variables that may influence the results. However, professional background and socialization may have an effect on cooperative behavior (Frank, Gilovich, & Regan, 1993).

Another important aspect to consider is the perception of the rules by participants. As the results showed, both groups, regardless whether they experienced imposed or self-chosen rules, perceived the rules itself as fair. Two possible explanations exist. At best the set of rules can be seen as 'good' governance rules influencing the game positively. In the worst case scenario the rules are perceived as unremarkable, since they do not influence the game significantly. In either case rules are perceived as fair, in the first case since rules were helpful, in the second case because they did not hinder the group. Considering the content analysis of the chat messages, I am inclined to believe in the former case as participants were in favor of one of the governance rules: they strongly urged for a project leader (rule 1). Nevertheless, both explanations may be true at the same time as some participants see one rule as helpful and another one as not noticeable. The question how much each explanation contributes is not of importance. Of importance is that more controversial rules may lead to different results. Controversial in the sense, that they conflict with the preferences of the group or may hinder them in their action. It is likely that such rules are perceived different, especially when imposed exogenously.

The mentioned limitations link to promising future research by replicating similar experiments over longer periods of time and across different, less homogenous groups or with more controversial set of rules. Furthermore it could be promising to counterpart findings from these studies with field research. Especially the relationship between different modes of governance and conflict seems a promising field to investigate.

For the things that have been mentioned may limit the generalization it is important to note, that overall the results prove to be of substance. I believe in the transferability of the results for manifold reasons. First, the design of the experiment was carefully chosen to rule out undesired effects as much as possible. The basic puzzle task was well established and is very generic, that is, it does not favor certain skills of participants (e.g. mathematical or language skills). Second, there were no signs for disrupting effects of variables not accounted for, as the inclusion of control variables showed. Third, the findings can be explained and correspond with existing theory. I therefore feel confident to draw conclusion and implications for research and practice from my results, always keeping in mind that any study is of limited scope.

7.3 Implications for Research

This dissertation thesis offers some insights on the effects of self- vs. firm-initiated governance of OCI communities, by the use of an experimental method. While questions about collaborative innovation projects have been mainly studied through case studies and surveys, I designed an experiment which I believe to be well fit to study OCI communities. Applying this research method I aim to contribute to narrow the criticized underrepresentation of experimental methods (Colquitt, 2008), especially when it comes to innovation research (Sørensen et al., 2010). The experimental task has proven to be very suitable, as it resembles the characteristics of OCI communities to a high degree. I therefore believe that the basic design is very appropriate to serve in future studies. One could conduct further experiments, for example investigating effects of different rule configurations, designing of longitude studies and exploring effects of more heterogeneous groups.

A further contribution for the future study of OCI communities is the application of the IAD framework. Part of the framework has been applied within the context of OSS communities (Schweik & Kitsing, 2010). Other authors have adapted the framework for OCI communities based on different case studies (cf. Madison et al., 2010). However, while the IAD framework is already well established for the study of communities managing CPRs, it takes future work to reach that status within the context of OCI. This dissertation tries to contribute to establish the IAD framework for the research of OCI communities, by expanding the application beyond case studies applying it for an experimental investigation.

With regard to the theory of transaction cost economics I contribute by highlighting the special characteristics of transactions within OCI communities. The asset being exchanged within OCI communities is mainly knowledge (e.g. specifications, source code, etc.), which differs significantly from other asset, in that it cannot be over exploited and that it must first be produced before in can be used (rather than natural resources). The special features of assets within the context of OCI relate exactly to the important aspect of asset specifity within TCE.

A further contribution with regard to TCE is the sharpening of behavioral assumptions of the involved actors. In addition to the two behavioral assumptions of TCE (bounded rationality and opportunism) I employed different theories and concepts rooted in social psychology. Blending theories of motivation with procedural justice and concepts of conflict within groups helps to improve understanding the complex nature of human interaction behavior in the context of OCI communities.

The studies contribute to better understand the relationship between external intervention, for example by firms, and communities of volunteers. First, the results of my experiment have shown that external intervention through governance rules does not per se cripple motivation of volunteers, but quite the opposite positive effects could be observed. If rules are perceived as helpful and fair, the may significantly reduce conflict and increase motivation. The interplay of key factors like justice, conflict and motivation within communities of volunteers is a further contribution of this study. Understanding this relationship provides insights for focusing on the right levers to increase motivation of volunteers.

I further showed the risks of the participation processes. While they may increase legitimacy they also inherent the risk of creating conflict and tension. Examples of endless 'vendettas' of *Wikipedia* volunteers deleting and reediting articles are living proof to that observation. We shall not be mistaken, democratic processes and participation of volunteers are important for such communities and probably key success factors. However, grass-root democratic processes can be a double-edged sword.

Several implications for the design of governance systems in communities and the interaction between exogenous actors and communities can be derived from the results. First, exogenous leadership by implementing governance structures may proof to be beneficial. A promising approach for leadership beyond pure structure is found by the involvement of firm employees acting as 'men on the inside' in such communities (Dahlander & Wallin, 2006; Lee et al., 2012). The next logical challenge is identifying a set of applicable fundamentals for 'good' governance rules that are perceived as tolerable and helpful by OCI communities. Again prior work by Ostrom may provide valuable insights. Ostrom (2003a) identified a set of different design principles to create successful self-organized regimes. Several principles correspond to the context of the production of knowledge resources by communities. In particular three principles stand out: First, balancing cost and benefits by designing rules to regulate the returns one receives for his inputs. Such principle is likely to mitigate the challenge of balancing use and production of knowledge resources (Madison et al., 2010). Second, accountability and enforcement of rules should be regulated by the community, increasing the perceived fairness and identification of the community with the rules. Third, sanctions should be applied gradually, depending on the seriousness of the rule violation. To further develop and adopt these principles to the special characteristics of OCI communities is a promising future research field.

As for governance, the concern that any external intervention may cripple motivation and reduce participation of volunteers should be reconsidered. The opposite may be the fact, where such external rules may proof to be a lever mitigating conflict and boosting the performance of such communities. However, this finding shall not be understood as a carte blanche for authoritarian external intervention. While such influence may be beneficial for a community, external governance rules still need to be designed in a careful manner. External rules can only succeed if they are perceived as fair and helpful and serve the purpose of the community. Maybe the initial question needs to be rephrased: The key of good governance lies not between endogenous vs. exogenous, but in the design of helpful, fair and purposeful governance rules and configurations. To investigate and find such configurations and processes to legitimize them is an avenue for further research.

7.4 Management Implications

As my research focus was the interaction of firm and community I want to conclude with some recommendations for managers of such firms. Recommendations of how a firm can establish a fruitful and sustainable cooperation with a community. I concluded my research implications saying that exogenous given rules can be beneficial, but that any external intervention must be approached with caution. I believe that following guidelines will help firms to develop such a fruitful affiliation with OCI communities.

Need for leadership

If a community is faced with the challenge to develop an innovative outcome members express a wish for structure and leadership. The importance of leadership for functioning groups and organizations is a known fact. What can be learned from my research is that communities have difficulties to establish a structure and appoint leadership. This is due the fact that community members have diverse preferences that may hinder a consensus. Bearing this finding in mind a firm should step into this power vacuum, by actively showing leadership. Leadership is best shown by the dedication of human resources and thought leadership. That is, beyond formulating rules for the community to follow, a firm should dedicate employees to actively work within the community. This strategy, known as a 'man on the inside' (MOI), has been already described and is promising for different reasons. First, leadership emerges naturally if a MOI proves to be competent. Community members turn to him for advice. Therefore leadership is perceived as fair and legitimated – a prerequisite for a functional governance system. Second, a firm can influence the direction of the community via the MOI. Once a MOI has gained a reputation and is perceived as legitimate it is easier to influence the direction of the community.

There are two important things for firms to consider when making use of employees within a community. First, such involvement comes not for free. In order to gain a standing and reputation considerable time is required by an employee. Dedicating few minutes per day is not enough. Second, they have to pick the right employee for the job. As for any profession working in a community requires a special skill set. Besides technical qualifications social skills are very important since communities are highly based on social relations rather than on strict hierarchies. This also relates to a third consideration. As social relations take a long time develop patience is needed until an employee has established himself within the community.

Structuring the democratic process

Letting a community participate in legislative processes in order to structure the governance of the community contains risks. The risk of disagreement among community members which may result in conflict and cripple motivation. However, democratic participation is necessary for establishing a trustful relationship between a firm and community. This risk is particularly high if the democratic process has no structure at all, for example a group discussion where everybody voices an opinion is likely to lead to chaos. For that reason it is necessary to structure such democratic processes in a way to benefit from the plus points and mitigate the risks. This is achieved by structuring the decision and discussion process in a way to moderate conflict, if it becomes counterproductive. Successful approaches could be drawn from political systems, for example having structured votes or discussions, where every individual voices its argument. Once again the employment of a MOI could be beneficial, since he could act as a moderator structuring controversial discussions. *Wikipedia* provides another example of structuring dissents by allowing users to comment and reedit articles. At the same time it provides some users with more rights, allowing them to end endless reediting vendettas.

No over regulation

Structure and governance within a community is important. However, an attempt by a firm to map its business rules and organization onto a community is likely to fail. A community consists of volunteers who are mainly intrinsically motivated and are not willing to find themselves in a strict hierarchical organization. A large part of interaction is based on informal norms and feelings of trust. A large set of rules entails the risk of crowding these established norms out and in consequence destroying the 'ecosystem' of a community. When it comes to rules within communities firms should pay attention to the principle "as little as possible, as much as necessary". A stepwise approach could be the right choice: Starting with few inevitable rules and adding new ones only if they seem necessary.

Choosing the right rules

When it comes to governance it is not only important to not 'over-regulate', but to choose the few rules carefully. Again resorting to the design principles of Ostrom (2000a), which were mentioned in the previous chapter, may help. Referring to these principles I identify three different types of rules, which I believe are helpful to structure successful communities.

Boundary rules – regulating access to the community

First boundary rules, regulating who is a member of the community are important. Such rules are likely to create a sense of belonging to the community. Another advantage of rules regulating who can be a member is that it helps to get the right people for the community. Other than for online communities producing simple outcomes, the production of complex goods, for example software, requires highly skilled volunteers. Some communities are well aware of this challenge and only allow full access if a volunteer proofs his skill in advance (Fang & Neufeld, 2009). Naturally this may limit the number of community members. Therefore the choice firms have to make is of strategic nature and highly dependent on their goal. A firm has to decide whether to pursue the aim of having a fast growing community and attract as many volunteers as possible or a community of highly skilled members.

Monitoring and conflict resolution

Communities highly depend on trust between community members. Therefore over formalized monitoring rules seem not imperative. Large scale monitoring also ties up resources, which cannot be dedicated to useful community work. Consequently monitoring should be not exerted by a dedicated role but rather on an informal basis by all community members. However, if a severe violation is reported, certain procedures to deal with the violation are necessary. Dedicated administrators warning or banning (based on the heaviness of the infringement) the violator are an example of such a procedure.

The procedure for dealing with violation of rules is closely linked to procedures for conflict mitigation. Conflict may not only occur if rules are violated, but also if different opinions clash. Again processes including moderators, trying to steer such controversies, could mitigate the rise of too much conflict. This is especially important, considering the effect high levels of conflict can have on factors like motivation, as shown in the previous studies.

Information rules – defining information flows and tools

Rules regulating information flows, that is, what is shared and how information is stored, are inseparable linked to technology. Technologies, namely internet based collaboration tools like chat rooms and wikis are not only the means by which communities interact but also determine how a community is structured. The way technology is applied directly impacts the organization of the community. For example the choice between a restricted mailing list and an open wiki is a technological and a governance choice at the same time. Firms should realize what information strategy to pursue, more precisely what information they want to share with the community, and then chose the right technology to support the choice. Considering the right choice I like to point to a recommendation made before: information rules and tools should be as simple and few regulated as possible. Choosing complex information rules, facilitated through a complex technology (e.g. different layers of access) are likely to hinder the collaboration and therefore the performance of a community. The way wikis in general are structured, are a fine example how to balance transparency and restriction of information within communities. Transparent, because prior information is always stored as an early version of a document, but at the same time it is administrators allowed overwrite incorrect articles.

The implementation of these recommendations requires substantial organizational change. Old habits and thought patterns have to be set aside. For instance firms have to formulate a new approach to intellectual property rights and grant employees who interact with communities some organizational slack to develop close relationships with the community. As for any organizational change managers will encounter refusal and resistance. To overcome these barriers is worthwhile, because much is to be gained by utilizing the endless pool of creativity and work resources of OCI communities.

APPENDIX

A. Instructions

Timeline and instructions for the experiment

Thank you for participating in this experiment. The experiment will last a little over one hour. Please take your time to read through the instructions. We will check on you after step 2.

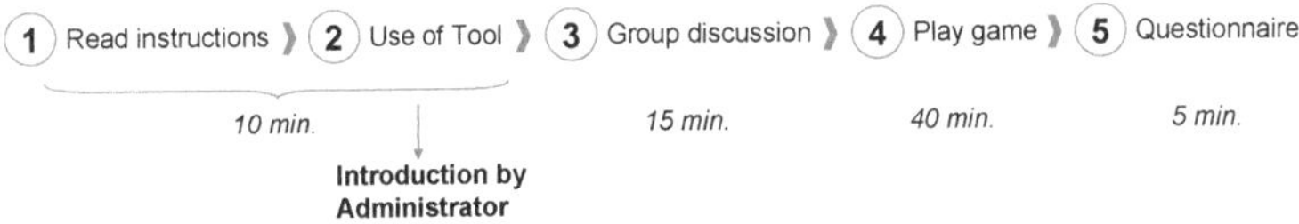

1 Instructions

Goal of the game

You are participating in a group puzzle exercise. **Goal of the game is to form your own square out of different puzzle pieces.** In order to form a square you have to exchange pieces with 4 other players who are participating in this game.

During this game you will be able to earn points, depending whether you **and** the other players in your group are able to form a square. The 5 players with the most points will receive an Amazon voucher worth 20€. There will be other groups of 5 playing this game. So your points are compared with your 4 group members and all players of the other 15 groups (see `Point allocation` section how points are allocated)

Procedure of game

Start:

At the beginning of the game every player has a set of pieces in his *Inboxes*. (The pieces will appear once the game is started, so the boxes are now empty)

Forming squares:

Within the *Inboxes* pieces can be rotated by double-clicking on them. In the upper left corner every player will find an individual *Solution box*. To form your own square you must move pieces from one of the *Inboxes* via drag-and-drop to the solution box. Within the *Solution box* pieces can be arranged freely (Do not worry too much about perfect alignment of pieces). The *Solution box* has the same measurements as your square must have.

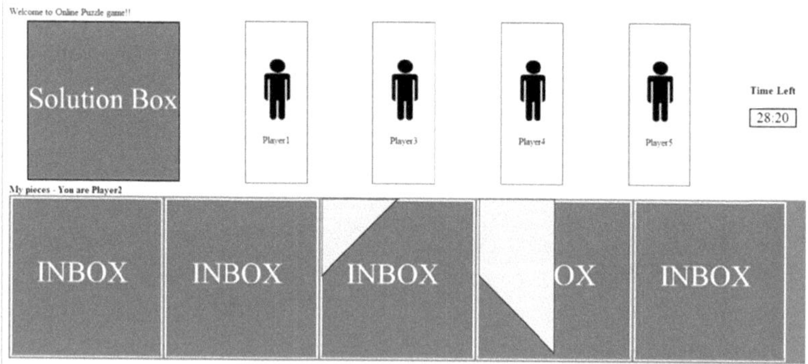

Exchanging Pieces:

In order to give pieces to other players you have to move the piece via drag-and-drop onto the player. Pieces you receive will appear in one of the *Inboxes*. Notice that you can only hold 5 pieces. If you reach that limit you are not able to receive further pieces.

Possible solutions:

Out of the pieces distributed among the 5 players squares can be formed in many ways. However if five squares must be constructed out of the pieces there is **only one**

arrangement that can succeed (5 squares are possible!). This also means, while you already accomplished a square, you might **block other solutions** if you do not have the perfect solution and are not willing to exchange pieces anymore.

Communication & time:

Once the game is started you will be able to chat via Skype with the other players. Do not use real names during the chat, address each other only by player number. You will have 40 minutes to solve the task. If you finish early you may signal this to the administrator who will end the game.

Point allocation

The allocation of points you receive depends on your individual **and** group performance. After 40 minutes there will be a count of how many squares your group was able to form (Counted are the squares in each *Solution box* – each player can only form one square). Based on the count each player will be given a number of points which are calculated by following formula:

20 points for your square + Number of total group squares (including your square) x 10 Points

Hence you can reach 0 to 70 points, depending on how many squares your group is able to form and whether your individual square Is among them. For demonstration payoff table below.

Number of total **group squares** formed

	0	1	2	3	4	5
Own square	N/A	30	40	50	60	70
No own square	0	10	20	30	40	N/A

Payoff Table

Remember that your points are also compared with other groups. If there are more than 5 participants with the same number of points, the group time needed to reach the solution will be taken into account.

Treatment A:

Before the 40 minutes are started by the administrator you have **15 minutes as a group to discuss a set of rules** (Step 3) that might help you to come to better results as a group. The list of rules will be given to you before the discussion starts.

Treatment B:

Before the 40 minutes are started by the administrator you have **15 minutes as a group to discuss any topic you like** (Step 3). During the 15 minutes the administrator will give you some more directions.

At the end of the game you will be asked to fill out a short survey.

Before the game is started the administrator will show how to use the tool. The key functions of the tool are also described under 2.

2   How to use the tool

Some basics on how to use the tool:

- You **can rotate pieces** that are in the "Inbox" by double clicking them (Notice: only in the " Inbox", so you have to move them there before you can exchange them)
- Notice that your "Inbox" **can only hold 5 pieces** at a time, this includes pieces which are currently in the "Solution Box (This also means a player with 5 pieces cannot receive further pieces)
- In order to form your square you have to drag pieces from your "Inbox" to the "Solution Box" in the upper left corner, and **arrange them** there
- If you want to move pieces from your "Solution box" back to your "Inbox" (for rotating or exchanging them), pay attention that you are only able to move them to **the box they came from**

- Pieces in your "Inbox" can be **given to participants via drag-and-drop** (click once on the piece, keep the mouse button pressed and drag in onto the participant you want to give the piece to)
- You may **communicate** via Skype chat with the other participants (Sign in will be given to you before the game)
- **No real names** are to be used, please address each other only by player 1 through 5
- **Do not close the browser**
- **Do not use the refresh button**

B. List of rules to choose from

Before you start to play the game you have to choose some rules that might help you perform better. Choose your rules carefully **they can affect the outcome** of the game significantly. For each block one rule has to be chosen. You have **15 minutes** to discuss the rules as a group and come to a consensus. At the end of the 15 minutes the administrator will ask the group via skype about the choice.

List of rules:

1. Project leader (keeps track of time, coordinates, solves issues, might have higher decision rights → see 2 d)

Do you choose to have a project leader

Yes   ☐

No   ☐

If you choose ´yes` please select an option

1a   A project leader is appointed by vote of the group.

1b   A project leader is appointed by fortune   (administrator determines him by fortune).

2. Decision rights for exchanging pieces

2a   No player can be forced to exchange/give away a piece.

2b   A player must exchange/give away a piece if the majority of a group requests it (3 players).

2c   A player must exchange/give away a piece if all other player request it (4 players).

2d   *The project leader can force a player to exchange a piece.*

Only applicable if a project leader is selected under 1

C. Questionnaire

After Game Survey

Thank you for participating in the game. You are nearly done, however before you leave please fill out this short survey. Please base all answers on **your personal point** of view and your experience **during** the game. (The group discussion at the beginning was also part of the game). Please also make use of the **full scale** available when answering the questions.

Please rate how you feel about the game? Please base you answer on your experience within the last 55 minutes. (Check only one box per row)

	extremely	quite	slightly	neutral	slightly	quite	extremely	
monotonous	☐	☐	☐	☐	☐	☐	☐	exciting
ordinary	☐	☐	☐	☐	☐	☐	☐	novel
unenjoyable	☐	☐	☐	☐	☐	☐	☐	enjoyable
painful	☐	☐	☐	☐	☐	☐	☐	pleasurable
monotonous	☐	☐	☐	☐	☐	☐	☐	challenging
boring	☐	☐	☐	☐	☐	☐	☐	interesting
disappointing	☐	☐	☐	☐	☐	☐	☐	promising
frustrating	☐	☐	☐	☐	☐	☐	☐	gratifying

To what extent did you observe following during the game?

	Not at all				To an exceptional degree
How much anger was there among the group during the game?	☐	☐	☐	☐	☐
How much personal friction was there in the group during the game?	☐	☐	☐	☐	☐
How much were personality clashes between group members evident during the game?	☐	☐	☐	☐	☐
How much tension was there in the group during the game?	☐	☐	☐	☐	☐
How many disagreements over different ideas about decisions and actions were there?	☐	☐	☐	☐	☐
How many differences about the content of decisions and actions did the group have to work through?	☐	☐	☐	☐	☐
How many differences of opinion were there within the group over actions and decisions?	☐	☐	☐	☐	☐

Suppose you have 40 units of something desirable to distribute across your team in proportion to their overall contribution, cooperation and effort during this game. Please distribute the units accordingly. (You must distribute <u>all</u> 40 units) *Please comment on the reasons if you reward some higher/lower than others.*

	number of units	*comment*
Player 2	__________	_________________________________
Player 3	__________	_________________________________
Player 4	__________	_________________________________
Player 5	__________	_________________________________

In the course of the game you had to obey some rules. Please rate how you experienced these rules or the actions resulting from these rules.

	Not at all				To an exceptional degree
Have you been able to express your views and feelings during those actions?	☐	☐	☐	☐	☐
Have you had influence over the outcome arrived at by those actions?	☐	☐	☐	☐	☐
Have those rules been applied consistently?	☐	☐	☐	☐	☐
Have those rules been free of bias?	☐	☐	☐	☐	☐

Please rate how you were treated by other players.

	Not at all				To an exceptional degree
Have they treated you in a polite manner?	☐	☐	☐	☐	☐
Have they treated you with dignity?	☐	☐	☐	☐	☐
Have they treated you with respect?	☐	☐	☐	☐	☐
Have they refrained from improper remarks or comments?	☐	☐	☐	☐	☐

In order to receive your credits and the potential prize please provide some information.

Name ____

Matrikelnummer ____

Age _______________

What is your native language

☐ German

☐ English

☐ Other → please specify _______________________________

What is you gender?

☐ Male

☐ Female

D. Statistical analysis

<u>MANCOVA</u>

Effect	Wilks' λ	F	df1	df2	Sig.
Typing Speed	.902	1.211	5	56	.316
Language	.927	.885	5	56	.497
Gender	.894	1.334	5	56	.264

REFERENCES

Adler, P. S. 2011. Perspective—The Sociological Ambivalence of Bureaucracy: From Weber via Gouldner to Marx. *Organization Science*.

Ajzen, I., & Fishbein, M. 1977. Attitude-behavior relations: A theoretical analysis and review of empirical research. *Psychological Bulletin*, 84(5): 888–918.

Alexy, O., & Leitner, M. 2010. A Fistful of Dollars: Financial Rewards, Payment Norms, and Motivation Crowding in Open Source Software Development. *SSRN eLibrary*.

Amason, A. C. 1996. Distinguishing the effects of functional and dysfunctional conflict on strategic decision making: resolving a paradox for top management teams. *Academy of Management Journal*, 39(1): 123–148.

Antikainen, M., Aaltonen, T., & Väisänen, J. 2007. The role of trust in OSS communities — Case Linux Kernel community: Open Source Development, Adoption and Innovation. In J. Feller, B. Fitzgerald, W. Scacchi & A. Sillitti (Eds.), vol. 234: 223–228: Springer Boston.

Aronson, E., Wilson, T. D., & Akert, R. M. 2010. *Sozialpsychologie* (6th ed.). München: Pearson Studium.

Backhaus, K. 2008. *Multivariate Analysemethoden: Eine anwendungsorientierte Einführung ; [Extras im Web]* (12th ed.). Berlin: Springer.

Baldwin, C. Y., & Clark, K. B. 2006. The Architecture of Participation: Does Code Architecture Mitigate Free Riding in the Open Source Development Model? *Management Science*, 52(7): 1116–1127.

Baldwin, C., & Hippel, E. von 2011. Modeling a Paradigm Shift: From Producer Innovation to User and Open Collaborative Innovation. *Organization Science*, 22(6): 1399–1417.

Bales, R. F. 1976. *Interaction process analysis: A method for the study of small groups.* Chicago: Univ. of Chicago Press.

Baron, R. M., & Kenny, D. A. 1986. The moderator–mediator variable distinction in social psychological research: Conceptual, strategic, and statistical considerations. *Journal of Personality and Social Psychology*, 51(6): 1173-1182.

Bavelas, A. 1950. Communication Patterns in Task-Oriented Groups. *Journal of the Acoustical Society of America*, 22(6): 725–730.

Becker, T. E. 2005. Potential Problems in the Statistical Control of Variables in Organizational Research: A Qualitative Analysis With Recommendations. *Organizational Research Methods*, 8(3): 274–289.

Bénabou, R., & Tirole, J. 2003. Intrinsic and Extrinsic Motivation. *The Review of Economic Studies*, 70(3): 489–520.

Benz, A., Lütz, S., Schimank, U., & Simonis, G. 2007. Einleitung. In A. Benz, S. Lütz, U. Schimank & G. Simonis (Eds.), *Handbuch Governance. Theoretische Grundlagen und empirische Anwendungsfelder*: 9–26. Wiesbaden: VS Verlag für Sozialwissenschaften / GWV Fachverlage GmbH Wiesbaden.

Bies, R. J., & Shapiro, D. L. 1987. Interactional fairness judgments: The influence of causal accounts. *Social Justice Research*, 1(2): 199–218.

Bogers, M., & West, J. 2012. Managing Distributed Innovation: Strategic Utilization of Open and User Innovation. *Creativity and Innovation Management*, 21(1): 61–75.

Bonaccorsi, A., & Rossi, C. 2003. Why Open Source software can succeed: Open Source Software Development. *Research Policy*, 32(7): 1243–1258.

Bonaccorsi, A., & Rossi, C. 2006. Comparing motivations of individual programmers and firms to take part in the open source movement: From community to business. *Knowledge, Technology & Policy*, 18(4): 40–64.

Boniface, D. R. 1995. *Experiment design and statistical methods: For behavioural and social research* (1st ed.). London: Chapman & Hall.

Bortz, J., & Weber, R. 2005. *Statistik für Human- und Sozialwissenschaftler: Mit 242 Tabellen* (6th ed.). Heidelberg: Springer Medizin.

Bowles, S., & Gintis, H. 2002. Social Capital and Community Governance. *Economic Journal*, 112(483): 419–436.

Brooks, C. M., & Ammons, J. L. 2003. Free Riding in Group Projects and the Effects of Timing, Frequency, and Specificity of Criteria in Peer Assessments. *Journal of Education for Business*, 78(5): 268–272.

Bühl, A. 2006. *SPSS 14: Einführung in die moderne Datenanalyse* (10th ed.). München: Pearson Studium.

Cameron, J., & Pierce, W. D. 1994. Reinforcement, Reward, and Intrinsic Motivation: A Meta-Analysis. *Review of Educational Research*, 64(3): 363–423.

Campbell, D. J. 1988. Task Complexity: A Review and Analysis. *Academy of Management Review*, 13(1): 40–52.

Capra, E., Francalanci, C., & Merlo, F. 2008. An Empirical Study on the Relationship Between Software Design Quality, Development Effort and Governance in Open Source Projects. IEEE Transactions on Software Engineering, 34: 765–782.

Cardenas, J.-C. 2004. Norms from outside and from inside: an experimental analysis on the governance of local ecosystems: Economics of Sustainable Forest Management. *Forest Policy and Economics*, 6(3-4): 229–241.

Carroll, G., & Teece, D. J. 1999. *Firms, markets, and hierarchies: The transaction cost economics perspective*. New York: Oxford University Press.

Cheliotis, G. 2009. From open source to open content: Organization, licensing and decision processes in open cultural production: Online Communities and Social Network. *Decision Support Systems*, 47(3): 229–244.

Chesbrough, H. 2006. *Open business models: How to thrive in the new innovation landscape*. Boston, Mass: Harvard Business School.

Chesbrough, H. W. 2003. *Open innovation: The new imperative for creating and profiting from technology*. Boston, Mass: Harvard Business School Press.

Chesbrough, H. W., & Appleyard, M. M. 2007. Open Innovation and Strategy. *California Management Review*, 50(1): 57–77.

Chesbrough, H. W., Vanhaverbeke, W., & West, J. 2008. *Open innovation: Researching a new paradigm*. Oxford: Oxford University Press.

Chiaburu, D. 2007. From Interactional Justice to Citizenship Behaviors: Role Enlargement or Role Discretion? *Social Justice Research*, 20(2): 207–227.

Colquitt, J. A. 2001. On the Dimensionality of Organizational Justice: A Construct Validation of a Measure. *Journal of Applied Psychology*, 86(3): 386–400.

Colquitt, J. A. 2008. From the Editors: Publishing Laboratory Research In AMJ: A Question of When, Not if. *Academy of Management Journal*, 51(4): 616–620.

Commons, J. R. 1990. *Institutional economics: Its place in political economy*. News Brunswick [N.J.] U.S.A: Transaction Publishers.

Cookson, R. 2000. Framing Effects in Public Goods Experiments. *Experimental Economics*, 3(1): 55–79.

Corfman, K. P., & Lehmann, D. R. 1987. Models of Cooperative Group Decision-Making and Relative Influence: An Experimental Investigation of Family Purchase Decisions. *Journal of Consumer Research*, 14(1): 1–13.

Crino, M. D., & White, M. C. 1982. Feedback Effects in Intrinsic/Extrinsic Reward Paradigms. *Journal of Management*, 8(2): 95–108.

D'Agostino, R. B., Belanger, A., & D'Agostino Jr., R. B. 1990. A Suggestion for Using Powerful and Informative Tests of Normality. *The American Statistician*, 44(4): 316–321.

Dahlander, L., & Gann, D. M. 2010. How open is innovation? *Research Policy*, 39(6): 699–709.

Dahlander, L., & Magnusson, M. 2008. How do Firms Make Use of Open Source Communities? *Long Range Planning*, 41(6): 629–649.

Dahlander, L., & Wallin, M. W. 2006. A man on the inside: Unlocking communities as complementary assets: Special issue commemorating the 20th Anniversary of David Teece's article, "Profiting from Innovation", in Research Policy. *Research Policy*, 35(8): 1243–1259.

Dahlander, L., Frederiksen, L., & Rullani, F. 2008. Online Communities and Open Innovation: Governance and Symbolic Value Creation. *Industry & Innovation*, 15(2): 115–123.

David, P. A., & Shapiro, J. S. 2008. Community-based production of open-source software: What do we know about the developers who participate?: Empirical Issues in Open Source Software. *Information Economics and Policy*, 20(4): 364–398.

Deci, E. L. 1971. Effects of Externally Mediated Rewards on Intrinsic Motivation. *Journal of Personality and Social Psychology*, 18(1): 105–115.

Deci, E. L., & Ryan, R. M. 1996. *Intrinsic motivation and self-determination in human behavior* (5th ed.). New York: Plenum Press.

Deci, E. L., Koestner, R., & Ryan, R. M. 1999. A meta-analytic review of experiments examining the effects of extrinsic rewards on intrinsic motivation. *Psychological Bulletin*, 125(6): 627–668.

Demil, B., & Lecocq, X. 2006. Neither Market nor Hierarchy nor Network: The Emergence of Bazaar Governance. *Organization Studies*, 27(10): 1447–1466.

DiStefano, C., Zhu, M., & Mindrila, D. 2009. Understanding and Using Factor Scores: Considerations for the Applied Researcher. *Practical Assessment, Resarch & Evaluation*, 14(20): 1–11.

Dixit, A. 2009. Governance Institutions and Economic Activity. *American Economic Review*, 99(1): 5–24.

Dreu, C. K. W. de 2006. When Too Little or Too Much Hurts: Evidence for a Curvilinear Relationship Between Task Conflict and Innovation in Teams. *Journal of Management*, 32(1): 83–107.

Dreu, C. K. W. de, & Weingart, L. R. 2003. Task versus relationship conflict, team performance, and team member satisfaction: A meta-analysis. *Journal of Applied Psychology*, 88(4): 741–749.

Economic Sciences Prize Committee of the Royal Swedish Academy of Sciences 2009. *Scientific Background on the Sveriges Riksbank Prize in Economic Sciences in Memory of Alfred Nobel 2009 ECONOMIC GOVERNANCE.*

Eisenhardt, K. M., & Schoonhoven, C. B. 1990. Organizational Growth: Linking Founding Team, Strategy, Environment, and Growth among U.S. Semiconductor Ventures, 1978-1988. *Administrative Science Quarterly*, 35(3): 504–529.

Fang, Y., & Neufeld, D. 2009. Understanding Sustained Participation in Open Source Software Projects. *Journal of Management Information Systems*, 25(4): 9–50.

Feldman, D. C. 2004. What are We Talking About When We Talk About Theory? *Journal of Management*, 30(5): 565–567.

Feller, J., & Fitzgerald, B. *Understanding Open Source Software development.* London ;, Boston: Addison-Wesley, c2002.

Fink, M. 2003. *The business and economics of Linux and open source.* Upper Saddle River, NJ: Prentice Hall PTR.

Fleming, L., & Waguespack, D. M. 2007. Brokerage, Boundary Spanning, and Leadership in Open Innovation Communities. *Organization Science*, 18(2): 165–180.

Fosfuri, A., Giarratana, M. S., & Roca, E. 2011. Community-focused strategies. *Strategic Organization*, 9(3): 222–239.

Frank, R. H., Gilovich, T., & Regan, D. T. 1993. Does Studying Economics Inhibit Cooperation? *The Journal of Economic Perspectives*, 7(2): 159–171.

Franke, N., & Shah, S. 2003. How communities support innovative activities: an exploration of assistance and sharing among end-users. *Research Policy*, 32(1): 157–178.

Frey, B. S. 1994. How Intrinsic Motivation is Crowded out and in. *Rationality and Society*, 6(3): 334–352.

Frey, B. S., & Jegen, R. 2000. Motivation Crowding Theory: A Survey of Empirical Evidence. *CESifo Working Paper Series*, 245.

Frey, B. S., & Jegen, R. 2001. Motivation Crowding Theory. *Journal of Economic Surveys*, 15(5): 589.

Füller, J. 2006. Why Consumers engage in virtual new Product Developments initiated by Producers. *Advances in Consumer Research*, 33(1): 639–646.

Füller, J., Jawecki, G., & Mühlbacher, H. 2007. Innovation creation by online basketball communities. *Journal of Business Research*, 60(1): 60–71.

Gagné, M., & Deci, E. L. 2005. Self-determination theory and work motivation. *J. Organiz. Behav.*, 26(4): 331–362.

Gassmann, O., Enkel, E., & Chesbrough, H. 2010. The future of open innovation. *R&D Management*, 40(3): 213–221.

Ghosh, R. A. 2005. Understanding Free Software Developers: Findings from the FLOSS Study. In J. Feller (Ed.), *Perspectives on free and open source software*: 23–46. Cambridge, Mass.: MIT Press.

Ghoshal, S., & Moran, P. 1996. Bad for practice: A critique of the transaction cost theory. *Academy of Management Review*, 21(1): 13–47.

Gladstein, D. L. 1984. Groups in Context: A Model of Task Group Effectiveness. *Administrative Science Quarterly*, 29(4): 499–517.

Green, S. G., & Taber, T. D. 1980. The effects of three social decision schemes on decision group process. *Organizational Behavior and Human Performance*, 25(1): 97–106.

Greenberg, J. 1987. A Taxonomy of Organizational Justice Theories. *Academy of Management Review*, 12(1): 9–22.

Greif, A. 1997. On the Social Foundations and Historical Development of Institutions that Facilitate Impersonal Exchange: From the Community Responsibility System to Individual Legal Responsibility in Pre-modern Europe. *Working paper, Department of Economics, Stanford University*.

Groenewegen, J. 1996. Transaction Cost Economics and Beyond: Why and How? In J. Groenewegen (Ed.), *Transaction cost economics and beyond*: 1–11. Boston: Kluwer Academic Publishers.

Hagel, J., & Armstrong, A. 1997. *Net gain: Expanding markets through virtual communities*. Boston: Harvard Business School Press.

Hair, J. F. 2010. *Multivariate data analysis: A global perspective* (7th ed.). Upper Saddle River, NJ: Pearson.

Hare, A. P. 1973. Theories of Group Development and Categories for Interaction Analysis. *Small Group Research*, 4(3): 259–304.

Harhoff, D., Henkel, J., & Hippel, E. von 2003. Profiting from voluntary information spillovers: how users benefit by freely revealing their innovations. *Research Policy*, 32(10): 1753–1769.

Hawkins, R. E. 2004. The economics of open source software for a competitive firm. *NETNOMICS*, 6(2): 103–117.

Heide, J. B. 1994. Interorganizational Governance in Marketing Channels. *The Journal of Marketing*, 58(1): 71–85.

Hellström, T. 2003. Governing the virtual academic commons. *Research Policy*, 32(3): 391–401.

Hippel, E. von 2001. Innovation by User Communities: Learning from Open-Source Software. (cover story). *MIT Sloan Management Review*, 42(4): 82–86.

Hippel, E. von 2006. *Democratizing innovation*. Cambridge, Mass, London: MIT Press.

Hippel, E. von, & von Krogh, G. 2003. Open Source Software and the 'Private-Collective' Innovation Model: Issues for Organization Science. *Organization Science*, 14(2): 209–223.

Hoegl, M., & Gemuenden, H. G. 2001. Teamwork Quality and the Success of Innovative Projects: A Theoretical Concept and Empirical Evidence. *Organization Science*, 12(4): 435–449.

Holland, R. W., Verplanken, B., & van Knippenberg, A. 2002. On the nature of attitude–behavior relations: the strong guide, the weak follow. *European Journal of Social Psychology*, 32(6): 869–876.

Howell, D. C. 2010. *Statistical methods for psychology* (7th ed.). Australia , Belmont CA: Thomson Wadsworth.

Isacc, R. M., & Walker, J. 1988. Communication and Free-Riding Behavior: The Voluntary Contribution Mechanism. *Economic Inquiry*, 26(4): 585–608.

Janssen, O. 2003. Innovative behaviour and job involvement at the price of conflict and less satisfactory relations with co-workers. *Journal of Occupational and Organizational Psychology*, 76(3): 347–364.

Janssen, O. 2004. How fairness perceptions make innovative behavior more or less stressful. *J. Organiz. Behav.*, 25(2): 201–215.

Jehn, K. A. 1995. A Multimethod Examination of the Benefits and Detriments of Intragroup Conflict. *Administrative Science Quarterly*, 40(2): 256–282.

Jenny, A., Hechavarria Fuentes, F., & Mosler, H.-J. 2007. Psychological Factors Determining Individual Compliance with Rules for Common Pool Resource Management: The Case of a Cuban Community Sharing a Solar Energy System. *Human Ecology*, 35(2): 239–250.

Jeppesen, L. B. O., & Molin, M. J. 2003. Consumers as Co-developers: Learning and Innovation Outside the Firm. *Technology Analysis & Strategic Management*, 15(3): 363.

Jeppesen, L. B., & Frederiksen, L. 2006. Why Do Users Contribute to Firm-Hosted User Communities? The Case of Computer-Controlled Music Instruments. *Organization Science*, 17(1): 45–63.

Jick, T. D. 1979. Mixing Qualitative and Quantitative Methods: Triangulation in Action. *Administrative Science Quarterly*, 24(4): 602–611.

Jones, C., Hesterly, W. S., & Borgatti, S. P. 1997. A general theory of network governance: exchange conditions and social mechanisms. *Academy of Management Review*, 22(4): 911–945.

Kannan, P. K., Chang, A.-M., & Whinston, A. B. 2000. Electronic Communities in E-Business: Their Role and Issues. *Information Systems Frontiers*, 1(4): 415–426.

Kaplan, M. F., & Miller, C. E. 1987. Group Decision Making and Normative Versus Informational Influence: Effects of Type of Issue and Assigned Decision Rule. *Journal of Personality and Social Psychology*, 53(2): 306–313.

Kassarjian, H. H. 1977. Content Analysis in Consumer Research. *Journal of Consumer Research*, 4(1): 8–18.

Katz, R., & Tushman, M. 1979. Communication patterns, project performance, and task characteristics: An empirical evaluation and integration in an R&D setting. *Organizational Behavior and Human Performance*, 23(2): 139–162.

Kent, R. A. 2001. *Data construction and data analysis for survey research*. Basingstoke, Hampshire: Palgrave.

Kerr, N. L., & Tindale, R. S. 2004. Froup performance and decision making. *Annual Review of Psychology*, 55(1): 623–655.

Kittur, A., & Kraut, R. (Eds.) 2010. *Beyond Wikipedia: Coordination and Conflict in Online Production Groups. {CSCW} 2010:* {ACM}.

Kollock, P., & Smith, M. Managing the virtual commons: cooperation and conflict in computer communities., *Proc. Computer-Mediated Communication: Linguistic, Social, and Cross-Cultural*, vol. 1996: 109–128.

Konovsky, M. A. 2000. Understanding Procedural Justice and Its Impact on Business Organizations. *Journal of Management*, 26(3): 489–511.

Kraus, S. J. 1995. Attitudes and the Prediction of Behavior: A Meta-Analysis of the Empirical Literature. *Personality and Social Psychology Bulletin*, 21(1): 58–75.

Krippendorff, K. 2009. *Content analysis: An introduction to its methodology* (2nd ed.). Thousand Oaks, Calif.: SAGE Publ.

Laat, P. B. de 2007a. Governance of open source software: state of the art. *Journal of Management and Governance*, 11(2): 165–177.

Laat, P. de 2007b. Introduction to a roundtable on the governance of open source software: particular solutions and general lessons. *Journal of Management and Governance*, 11(2): 115–117.

Lakhani, K. R., & Hippel, E. von 2003. How open source software works: "free" user-to-user assistance. *Research Policy*, 32(6): 923–943.

Lakhani, K. R., & Wolf, R. G. 2005. Why hackers do what they do: Understanding motivation and effort in free/open source software projects. In J. Feller (Ed.), *Perspectives on free and open source software*: 3–22. Cambridge, Mass.: MIT Press.

Lattemann, C. 2007. Forschungsfeld Governance. In D. Wagner (Ed.), *Governance-Theorien oder Governance als Theorie?*: 29–62. Berlin: WVB Wiss. Verl. Berlin.

Lattemann, C., & Stieglitz, S. 2005. Framework for Governance in Open Source Communities. *Proceedings of the 38th Hawaii International Conference on System Sciences*: 1–11.

Laursen, K., & Salter, A. 2006. My Precious Technology: The Role of Legal Appropriability Strategy in Shaping Innovative Performance. *Working Paper. Tanaka Business School, Imperial College London*.

Lee, G. K., & Cole, R. E. 2003. From a Firm-Based to a Community-Based Model of Knowledge Creation: The Case of the Linux Kernel Development. *Organization Science*, 14(6): 633–649.

Lee, V., Herstatt, C., & Husted, K. 2012. *How firms can strategically influence open source communities: The employment of 'men on the inside'*. Techn. Univ., Institut für Technologie- und Innovationsmanagement, Diss.--Hamburg-Harburg, 2011. (1st ed.). Wiesbaden: Gabler.

Lerner, J., & Tirole, J. 2001. The open source movement: Key research questions: 15th Annual Congress of the European Economic Association. *European Economic Review*, 45(4-6): 819–826.

Lerner, J., & Tirole, J. 2002. Some Simple Economics of Open Source. *Journal of Industrial Economics*, 50(2): 197.

Leventhal, G. S. 1980. What should be done with equity theory? New approaches to the study of fairness in social relationships. In K. J. Gergen (Ed.), *Social exchange. Advances in theory and research*: 27–55. New York: Plenum Press.

Lewis-Beck, M. S. 1994. *Factor analysis and related techniques*. London: SAGE.

Lüer, G., & Becker, D. 1987. *Allgemeine experimentelle Psychologie: Eine Einführung in die methodischen Grundlagen mit praktischen Übungen für das experimentelle Praktikum ; 84 Tabellen.* Stuttgart: Fischer.

Madison, M. J., Frischmann, B. M., & Strandburg, K. J. 2010. Constructing Commons in the Cultural Environment. *Cornell Law Review*, 95: 657–710.

Maio, G. R., & Haddock, G. 2009. *The psychology of attitudes and attitude change.* London ;, Los Angeles: SAGE.

Markus, L. 2007. The governance of free/open source software projects: monolithic, multidimensional, or configurational? *Journal of Management and Governance*, 11(2): 151–163.

Markus, M. L., Manville, B., & Agres, C. E. 2000. What Makes a Virtual Organization Work? *Sloan Management Review*, 42(1): 13–26.

Markus, U. 2002. *Integration der virtuellen Community in das CRM: Konzeption, Rahmenmodell, Realisierung.* Lohmar: Eul.

Micceri, T. 1989. The unicorn, the normal curve, and other improbable creatures. *Psychological Bulletin*, 105(1): 156–166.

Miles, J., & Shevlin, M. 2008. *Applying regression & correlation: A guide for students and researchers.* London: SAGE Publ.

Miller, C. E. 1985. Group Decision Making under Majority and Unanimity Decision Rules. *Social Psychology Quarterly*, 48: 51–61.

Millsap, R. E., & Maydeu-Olivares, A. 2009. *The SAGE handbook of quantitative methods in psychology.* Los Angeles: SAGE.

Mitchel, T. R., & Daniels, D. 2003. Motivation. In I. B. Weiner (Ed.), *Handbook of psychology*, vol. 12: 225–254. Hoboken, NJ: Wiley.

Neuendorf, K. A. 2010. *The content analysis guidebook* (9th ed.). Thousand Oaks: SAGE Publ.

Nonnecke, B. & Preece, J. 2000. Lurker demographics: counting the silent, *Proceedings of the SIGCHI conference on Human factors in computing systems*, 73–80. The Hague, The Netherlands: ACM.

North, D. C. 1990. *Institutions, institutional change, and economic performance.* Cambridge ;, New York: Cambridge University Press.

O'Mahony, S. 2007. The governance of open source initiatives: what does it mean to be community managed? *Journal of Management and Governance*, 11(2): 139–150.

O'Mahony, S. &. West. J.(2005) What makes a project open source? Migrating from organic to synthetic communities. *Paper presented at the Academy of Management Meeting (2006).*

O'Mahony, S., & Ferraro, F. 2007. The emergence of governance in an open source community. *Academy of Management Journal*, 50(5): 1079–1106.

Ostrom, E. 1999. Coping with tragedies of the commons. *Annual Review of Political Science*, 2(1): 493–535.

Ostrom, E. 2000a. Collective Action and the Evolution of Social Norms. *Journal of Economic Perspectives*, 14(3): 137–158.

Ostrom, E. 2000b. Crowding out Citizenship. *Scandinavian Political Studies*, 23(1): 3–16.

Ostrom, E. 2005. *Understanding institutional diversity.* Princeton, NJ: Princeton Univ. Press.

Ostrom, E. 2006. The value-added of laboratory experiments for the study of institutions and common-pool resources. *Journal of Economic Behavior & Organization,* 61(2): 149–163.

Ostrom, E. 2007. Challenges and growth: the development of the interdisciplinary field of institutional analysis. *Journal of Institutional Economics,* 3(03): 239–264.

Ostrom, E. 2010. Response: The Institutional Analysis and Development Framework and the Commons. *Cornell Law Review,* 95: 807.

Pierre, J., & Peters, B. G. 2000. *Governance, politics and the state.* Basingstoke: Macmillan [u.a.].

Podsakoff, P. M., Ahearne, M., & MacKenzie, S. B. 1997. Organizational citizenship behavior and the quantity and quality of work group performance. *Journal of Applied Psychology,* 82(2): 262–270.

Postmes, T., Spears, R., & Lea, M. 2000. The formation of group norms in computer-mediated communication. *Human Communication Research,* 26(3): 341–371.

Priem, R. L., & Harrison, D. A. 1995. Structured Conflict and Consensus Outcomes in Group Decision Making. *Journal of Management,* 21(4): 691–710.

Raasch, C., Herstatt, C., & Balka, K. 2009. On the open design of tangible goods. *R&D Management,* 39(4): 382–393.

Regan, D. T., & Fazio, R. 1977. On the consistency between attitudes and behavior: Look to the method of attitude formation. *Journal of Experimental Social Psychology,* 13(1): 28–45.

Rickartds, T. 1985. *Stimulating innovation: A system approach:* Palmer.

Roberts, P. W., & Greenwood, R. 1997. Integrating Transaction Cost and Institutional Theories: Toward a Constrained-Efficiency Framework for Understanding Organizational Design Adoption. *Academy of Management Review,* 22(2): 346–373.

Roberts, J. A., Il-Horn Hann, & Slaughter, S. A. 2006. Understanding the Motivations, Participation, and Performance of Open Source Software Developers: A Longitudinal Study of the Apache Projects. *Management Science,* 52(7): 984–999.

Ruef, M. 1996. The evolution of convention: Conformity and innovation in task-oriented networks. *Computational & Mathematical Organization Theory,* 2(1): 5–28.

Ryan, R. M., & Deci, E. L. 2000. Intrinsic and Extrinsic Motivations: Classic Definitions and New Directions. *Contemporary Educational Psychology,* 25(1): 54–67.

Santos, F. M., & Eisenhardt, K. M. 2005. Organizational Boundaries and Theories of Organization. *Organization Science,* 16(5): 491–508.

Sapienza, H. J., & Korsgaard, M. A. 1996. Procedural justice in entrepreneur-investor relations. *Academy of Management Journal,* 39(3): 544–574.

Schuppert, G. F. 2008. Governance - auf der Suche nach Konturen eines "anerkannt uneindeutigen Begriffs". In G. F. Schuppert & M. Zürn (Eds.), *Governance in einer sich wandelnden Welt:* 13–40 (1st ed.). Wiesbaden: VS Verlag für Sozialwissenschaften / GWV Fachverlage GmbH Wiesbaden.

Schweiger, D. M., Sandberg, W. R., & Ragan, J. W. 1986. Group approaches for improving strategic decision making: a comparative analysis of dialectical inquiry, devil's advocacy, and consensus. *Academy of Management Journal*, 29(1): 51–71.

Schweik, C. M., & Kitsing, M. 2010. Applying Elinor Ostrom's Rule Classification Framework to the Analysis of Open Source Software Commons. *Transnational Corporations Review*, 2(1): 13–26.

Shah, S. K. 2006. Motivation, Governance, and the Viability of Hybrid Forms in Open Source Software Development. *Management Science*, 52(7): 1000–1014.

Shelanski, H. A., & Klein, P. G. 1995. Empirical Research in Transaction Cost Economics: A Review and Assessment. *Journal of Law, Economics, & Organization*, 11(2): 335–361.

Shepperd, J. A. 1993. Productivity loss in performance groups: A motivation analysis. *Psychological Bulletin*, 113(1): 67–81.

Sidahmed, M., & Gerlach, J. Governance of Collaborative Open Source Software: Inference from Transaction Cost Economics Model; http://aisel.aisnet.org/cgi/viewcontent.cgi?article=1319&context=amcis2009, 06 May 2010.

Solum, L. B. 2005. Procedural Justice. *University of San Diego Law and Economics Research Paper Series*, 12: 178–322.

Sørensen, F., Mattsson, J., & Sundbo, J. 2010. Experimental methods in innovation research. *Research Policy*, 39(3): 313–322.

Spector, P. E., & Brannick, M. T. 2011. Methodological Urban Legends: The Misuse of Statistical Control Variables. *Organizational Research Methods*, 14(2): 287–305.

Stevens, C. K. 2011. Questions to Consider When Selecting Student Samples. *Journal of Supply Chain Management*, 47(3): 19–21.

Stock, R. M., & Hoyer, W. D. 2005. An Attitude-Behavior Model of Salespeople's Customer Orientation. *Journal of the Academy of Marketing Science*, 33(4): 536–552.

Streeck, W., & Schmitter, P. C. 1985. Community, Market, State-and Associations? The Prospective Contribution of Interest Governance to Social Order. *European Sociological Review*, 1(2): 119–138.

Sulin, B. 2001. Establishing online trust through a community responsibility system. *Decision Support Systems*, 31(3): 323–336.

Tapscott, D., & Williams, A. D. 2008. *Wikinomics: How mass collaboration changes everything*. New York: Portfolio.

Tenenberg, J. 2008. An institutional analysis of software teams: Collaborative and social aspects of software development. *International Journal of Human-Computer Studies*, 66(7): 484–494.

The American Heritage dictionary. The American Heritage dictionary; http://ahdictionary.com/word/search.html?q=theory, 14 Feb 2012.

Tietjen, M. A., & Myers, R. M. 1998. Motivation and job satisfaction. *Management Decision*, 36(4): 226–231.

Torre, A. 2006. Collective action, governance structure and organizational trust in localized systems of production. The case of the AOC organization of small producers. *Entrepreneurship & Regional Development*, 18(1): 55–72.

Tyler, T. R. 2005. Psychological Perspectives on Legitimacy and Legitimation: Annual Review of Psychology. *Annu. Rev. Psychol.*, 57(1): 375–400.

Tyler, T. R. 2006. *Why people obey the law.* Princeton, N.J.: Princeton University Press.

Ulhøi, J. P. 2004. Open source development: a hybrid in innovation and management theory. *Management Decision,* 42(9): 1095–1114.

Vallance, R., Kiani, S., & Nayfeh, S. (Eds.) 2001. *Open design of manufacturing equipment.*

van Dijk, E., & Wilke, H. 1995. Coordination Rules in Asymmetric Social Dilemmas: A Comparison between Public Good Dilemmas and Resource Dilemmas. *Journal of Experimental Social Psychology,* 31(1): 1–27.

van Rijnsoever, F. J., Meeus, M. T., & Donders, A. R. T. 2012. The effects of economic status and recent experience on innovative behavior under environmental variablity: An experimental approach. *Research Policy.*

von Krogh, G., & Hippel, E. von 2006. The Promise of Research on Open Source Software. *Management Science,* 52(7): 975–983.

Walker, H. A., Thomas, G. M., & Zelditch, M., JR 1986. Legitimation, Endorsement, and Stability. *Social Forces,* 64(3): 620–643.

Walker, O. C., Churchill, G. A., JR, & Ford, N. M. 1977. Motivation and Performance in Industrial Selling: Present Knowledge and Needed Research. *Journal of Marketing Research (JMR),* 14(2).

Wall, V. D., & Nolan, L. L. 1986. Perceptions of Inequity, Satisfaction, and Conflict in Task-Oriented Groups. *Human Relations,* 39(11): 1033–1051.

Walter, L., & Möhrle, M. G. 2009. Gestaltungsoptionen bei Geschäftsprozess-Patenten. In M. G. Möhrle & L. Walter (Eds.), *Patentierung von Geschäftsprozessen. Monitoring, Strategien, Schutz:* 41–74. Berlin ;, New York: Springer-Verlag.

Weber, M. 1978. *Economy and society: An outline of interpretive sociology.* Berkeley: University of California Press.

West, J., & Bogers, M. 2010. Contrasting Innovation Creation and Commercialization within Open, User and Cumulative Innovation. *Presented at the Academy of Management,* August.

West, J., & Lakhani, K. R. 2008. Getting Clear About Communities in Open Innovation. *Industry & Innovation,* 15(2): 223–231.

West, J., & O'Mahony, S. 2008. The Role of Participation Architecture in Growing Sponsored Open Source Communities. *Industry & Innovation,* 15(2): 145–168.

Wicker, A. W. 1969. Attitudes versus Actions: The Relationship of Verbal and Overt Behavioral Responses to Attitude Objects. *Journal of Social Issues,* 25(4): 41–78.

Willer, D., & Walker, H. A. 2007. *Building experiments: Testing social theory.* Stanford, Calif.: Stanford Social Sciences.

Williamson, O. E. 1981. The Economics of Organization: The Transaction Cost Approac. *American Journal of Sociology,* 87(3): 548–577.

Williamson, O. E. 1989. Transaction cost economics. In R. Schmalensee & R. Willig (Eds.), *Handbook of Industrial Organization, vol 1,* vol. 1: 135–182 (1st ed.).

Williamson, O. E. 1998. Transaction Cost Economics: How It Works; Where It is Headed. *De Economist,* 146(1): 23–58.

Williamson, O. E. 2005. The Economics of Governance. *American Economic Review*, 95(2): 1–18.

Wright, D. B., & London, K. 2009. *Modern Regression Techniques Using R: A Practical Guide for Students and Researchers*. London: Sage Publications.

Ying, L., & Salomo, S. 2011. Governance of Virtual Communities: A Literature Review and a Conceptual Framework. In E. J. Hultink (Ed.), *18th International Product Development Management Conference. "Innovate Through Design"*: 1–40.

Zwass, V. 2010. Co-Creation: Toward a Taxonomy and an Integrated Research Perspective. *International Journal of Electronic Commerce*, 15(1): 11–48.